SHADOWS ON THE WALL

SHADOWS ON THE WALL

STAN KRASNOFF

SHADOWS ON THE WALL

ALLEN&UNWIN

First published in 2002

Copyright © Stan Krasnoff 2002

Allen & Unwin
83 Alexander Street
Crows Nest NSW 2065
Australia
Phone: (61 2) 8425 0100
Fax: (61 2) 9906 2218
Email: info@allenandunwin.com
Web: www.allenandunwin.com

National Library of Australia
Cataloguing-in-Publication entry:

Krasnoff, Stan, 1939- .
  Shadows on the wall.

  ISBN 1 86508 887 0.

  1. Krasnoff, Stan, 1939- . 2. Tet Offensive, 1968 -
Personal narratives, Australian. 3. Vietnamese Conflict,
1961-1975 - Campaigns. I. Title.

959.70434

Set in 11/14 pt Sabon by Bookhouse, Sydney

10 9 8 7 6 5 4 3 2 1

WAY OF THE WARRIOR
FOREWORD

BY BO GRITZ

God be praised we are not all the same, but even as some animals migrate instinctively and others become food, a few of us are born with a heart like Samson and David and bred to be warriors. As the merchant lusts for gold, so my kind savours the sweetness of fighting death hand-to-hand and winning against all odds. This is a book about the rare few who were born to fight and were somehow allowed to come together for an all too brief period to claim their destiny.

For certain, there is a wide gulf between true warriors and plain soldiers. The latter dress in crisp uniforms and bask in books of regulations, marching bands and parade-ground brass. The warrior knows no rule book, hates neckties and sticks to his own. In battle, the warrior performs battlefield miracles on demand with audacity, bravery, and brutality. Warriors are the ones from whom the impossible is expected; these are forever brothers. They come to prove and fulfill their earthly purpose. Loving life, they are willing to die for that which they love more—each other, and their foreordained heritage!

God graced me as a fighter. As a teenager with appointments to several military colleges, I became impatient and enlisted.

SHADOWS ON THE WALL

My intention was to join the Para-Marines, but the recruiter was out to lunch and I noticed a poster in the Army office showing twelve men in battle gear bearing the slogan: *The Green Bereted Special Forces are the World's Toughest Troopers!* I joined. Paratroops, rangers, flying, and frogmen, I couldn't get enough! Special Forces became my beloved mistress. I became an officer so I could love her even more. Then came Vietnam. I couldn't wait. I volunteered, fearing the war would be over before I could be tested. Soon afterwards I was issued with emergency orders to replace a province intelligence officer who had been killed. The 5th Special Forces Group was ordered to Vietnam at the same time. I was heartbroken.

At a Friday night Hail & Farewell officers' call, General William P. Yarborough asked how I felt about my assignment. I explained it was like unhooking and sitting down just as my stick stood up to jump from the plane. My mentor told me to check with him the next morning before departing. I had already been told by a Pentagon friend that not even the President could change my priority assignment. My bags packed, I entered the World War II wooden Special Warfare Center Headquarters and came face-to-face with one of the meanest men in special forces, Colonel William P. 'Pappy' Grieves, the Chief of Staff. 'What do you want?' he snapped.

'I'm here to see General Yarborough about my assignment.'

'That won't be necessary. You're not going!'

'Not going with SF?'

'No! You're not going as an intelligence replacement. The General called Washington this morning and had your orders changed. As of now, you're an A-Team leader with the 5th Group. Now get out of here and quit causing so much trouble!'

I loved General Yarborough. He had been the Army's Intelligence Chief, designed the US Paratrooper Wings, negotiated the Korean armistice, and persuaded President John

Kennedy to authorize the Green Beret for Special Forces. Now he had made it possible for me to take my mistress to war.

My head aches with the volume of stories I have stored, and my heart swells with the memories of my fellow warriors, some of whom died in action and others who were maimed as a result of the many operations I conducted in the service of my country. But my job here is to set the scene for a series of missions called Project Rapid Fire, the essence of which was always the courage shown by my warriors, of whom Stan Krasnoff was one, and the faith they had in me. I can proudly say that I have never let them down, and I pray to God in thanks for His munificence in providing me with the character needed to lead not just men, but true warriors.

As soon as I think of Rapid Fire, my thoughts lead back to Blackjack Kelly.

The best of 5th Group's COs was Colonel Francis J. 'Blackjack' Kelly. Kelly was a big tough man who believed in telling his officers what to do, not how to do it.

It wasn't long before Kelly called me to his office.

'Do you see that map?' Col. Kelly was pointing at the center of War Zone C between what was known as the 'Fishhook' and the 'Elephant's Ear.' 'What would you say if I told you to take an A-Team and 100 guerrillas into there and stay for an indefinite period of time with no conventional support?'

My answer was immediate: 'I would say it would be suicide! War Zone C is flat, and full of both Communist regulars and VC. A force of 100 men could not outrun the enemy. The terrain would not support such an operation without the local support normally available to guerrillas.'

Kelly studied my response and remarked that I had been in that area with Delta more than anyone else, and that he valued my opinion. Had I saluted, done an about face (which I did) and walked out without another word, I would never have known the sweet and heady nectar of a warrior's Valhalla.

Eagles aren't supposed to flock, but they were already gathering. At the door, I turned and spoke one more sentence: 'If you ever get serious about somebody going in there, I guess it ought to be me.' Kelly didn't say a thing.

A week later I was again summoned to his office. The conversation was both terse and pithy. 'You have any questions?'

'About what, Sir?'

'About that!' he said, pointing to the map of War Zone C.

'Yes Sir! I don't have men, materials or mercenaries!'

'Those are problems for you to solve. I'm not interested in problems, just questions!'

'No Sir.'

'Alright then. Get out of here, come back and tell me what it was like. Westmoreland says you can have your choice of assignment at mission's end.'

Now this was a true SF mission—and if executed right we would do more than just shoot back!

War Zone C was the greater part of Tay Ninh Province, located against the Cambodian border and 125 kilometers northwest of Saigon. The C-Team controlling Tay Ninh Province was located at Bien Hoa, 25 kilometers northeast of Saigon, and was under the command of Lt. Col. Tom Huddleston. With nothing more than a verbal order from Kelly, I reported to Huddleston, telling him only that I was working a special mission for Blackjack Kelly and I needed his facilities. At first he was a little huffy, but when Kelly's name came up he became more helpful.

First, I put out a call all over Vietnam for SF volunteers interested in a one-time special operation that had never before been attempted. Next, I went to see a close friend, Major Dick Reish, CO of Project Sigma, a later southern augmentation to Delta. Reish ran his secret base out of Ho Ngoc Tao between Bien Hoa and Saigon. Dick already had secure ground, firing ranges, and plenty of space. I asked him for enough room to hold 300 Cambodians behind rolls of concertina-wire, plus my augmented A-Team. He was happy to help.

My new A-Team would be designated SFOD-A-303, and the Task Force would be codenamed Mobile Guerilla TF-957 (the three numbers equaling 21—a winner at blackjack). I ordered 300 M-2 carbines with 30-round magazines and 24, 1919-A-6 machine guns with ammunition from the logistical center at Nha Trang. We would soon open for business.

Even the Cambodes were excited when the twin-engine C-2 Caribou landed, bringing their weapons and tiger-striped uniforms – until the crates were opened. Instead of automatic-firing carbines, we had M-3 'grease-guns', and jungle boots and tiger suits had turned into Bata boots (tennis shoes) and green fatigues normally issued to regular CIDG strikers. I was pissed! I climbed aboard the big Army transport and returned with them to the SF headquarters.

I knocked on Kelly's closed door and heard his irritated growl to enter. Inside, I didn't give him the chance to play the heavy. 'Look, Sir, you gave me an all but impossible mission with no help thus far. We've stolen everything needed to build a camp. I asked you for carbines with 30-round magazines and you sent me grease guns with no magazines. How am I supposed to teach Cambodes how to shoot with single shot .45 M-3s? I need my SF to blend in with the guerrilla force, but I get green tennis shoes and fatigues. We are going to do what you asked, but are you going to help? That's a question, not a problem, Sir!'

'Get out of here,' Kelly boomed. 'Start walking toward the LSC. You'll be met!'

About half way to the Logistical Support Centre with its sprawling supply yards, docks and warehouses, I spied a lieutenant colonel in a puffing dog-trot, followed closely by a chief warrant officer and a master sergeant. 'Captain Gritz? I'm the Officer in Charge of the LSC. Colonel Kelly called to say that we had mis-sent you some supplies. If you will please let us know how we can help you, we'll have a plane loaded tonight and you can accompany it to your camp tomorrow morning. I believe you were interested in carbines and 30 caliber machine guns?' It was about to become Christmas.

'No Sir, I need 300 M-16 rifles, 24 M-60 machine guns, 24 M-79, 40 mm grenade launchers with ammo.' The warrant officer started to remind his boss that indigenous forces were not allowed to use the current American issue weapons, but the logistics chief barked, 'Give them to him! And give him 300 sets of tiger camos and the same number of US jungle boots.' Again, I heard the warrant start, but the Colonel, now in a sweat, interrupted with the same command: 'Give them to him!' As I turned to go, I caught a glimpse of what looked like Blackjack Kelly disappearing around the corner, and understood why the LSC couldn't say no.

Trained, organized, and equipped, we needed a good shake down. I arranged a launch out of the Duc Phuong A-camp near War Zone D. On the eve of the operation, Kelly showed up with Major James Van Strien, a Group Operations Officer. Kelly was all grins. He pulled me aside, looped his huge arm around my shoulders, looked around to make sure that no one was listening, and said in a low voice, 'When are we going?' I could tell he knew something that I should have known, but didn't.

'Sir? Going? You mean on our shake-down outside of Duc Phuong?'

Like a sudden storm at sea, Kelly's countenance darkened. Scowling at me he hissed, 'No, damn it! When are you going after the box?' I confessed I knew nothing about any 'box.'

Kelly now turned like an angry dragon on Van Strien, who was standing by, but keeping his distance. 'VAN STRIEN! DID YOU GIVE GRITZ THE MISSION I ORDERED?' Van, clearly at ground zero with no time left before detonation, gushed out a torrent of excuses, each one worse than the one before. He hit bottom with, 'But Sir, it would be like looking for a needle in a haystack.'

It was clearly the wrong thing to say. Kelly erupted! The eagles on his collar and beret accentuated his six-foot-three inch frame, and seemed to scream with him, 'DON'T YOU TALK TO ME ABOUT NEEDLES!'

The last I saw of Van Strien, ever, was his disappearance into the resident A-team's communication bunker with Kelly beating him over the head with his clipboard.

Kelly re-emerged and came for me, still in a rage. 'Briefers will be here immediately. This is above Top Secret, but I know you can do it. This is the highest priority. I want you in the field ASAP—and don't come back without that BOX! Is that CLEAR?'

The 'box' was a newly developed electronic counter-measure 13A system. The super-secret set of electronics, developed by Sanders Associates, deceived enemy anti-aircraft missile radar into believing the spy plane was in a position that it was not. If this technology was compromised our strategic reconnaissance aircraft could be accurately targeted. So there was good reason for the White House and Pentagon to insist that the box be recovered—at all costs.

The USAF briefing team arrived in short order. Engineers had pinpointed an area 25 miles wide and 25 miles long as the most likely crash sight—dead center in a denied area known to contain large enemy units. The cargo was considered so precious that no one on the ground search unit could know what it looked like! The box was less than a yard long, some three inches high, and eight inches wide, wrapped in battery operated, light-colored non-explosive incendiary panels.

As God would have it, MGTF-957 blundered onto the bird on the third day. It had pancaked into the triple canopy growth, which had absorbed much of the impact and left it sitting right side up. A minor fire had occurred and some compressor blades were visible through torn skin covering the Pratt & Whitney

J-75 engine. There was just one thing wrong – the tail and 13A system were missing, and the area was covered in Ho Chi Minh, BF Goodrich sandal prints. Clearly we weren't the first to visit the crash site. We destroyed the camera equipment, which could record a strip of earth 125 miles wide and 3 000 miles long with such clarity that you could read newspaper headlines, and assumed that the 13A system was lost forever. But as luck would have it one of Yed's patrol happened upon the box!

Up to that point we had carefully avoided enemy contact, but now we were compelled to show our hand. We ambushed a column attempting to take prisoners and killed them all. We then booby-trapped the bodies knowing that a recovery unit would soon appear. We captured two of the reinforcements. One was a private, probably 18 years young; the other was a hard-as-nails sergeant. Nothing could be done to gain his cooperation. On the other hand, the young soldier had a large piece of shrapnel lodged in his forehead and was cooperative. There was no way of sending them back for further interview.

I wish I could have pinned a medal on the enemy sergeant— he deserved it. Instead, in front of his subordinate, I gave him one more chance to help us. When he refused, I shot him dead. As my medic sought to treat the terrified private, I ordered him away, took a mirror and showed the soldier how bad he looked. I explained that we were guerrillas in a denied area with limited food and no means to safeguard prisoners. The only way his life would be spared was to be helpful. I promised that if he would do his best to help us, I would do my best to keep him alive. He saw the light.

I tied a noose of detonating cord around his neck and attached an electric blasting cap from a Claymore mine to it. He was our point. The first hostile gunshot, or attempt to warn his comrades, would result in my squeezing the hand-held clacker, sending his head up like a champagne cork.

I figured he would escape during the furor of the raid, but

as we pulled out through our security screen there he was, tagging along close to me. That night I tied him with parachute cord around a tree close to my hammock. I glanced at my watch and saw that it was midnight, Christmas morning. There was a truce for everyone engaged in the Vietnam War—except us. At that moment I heard a 'thunk' that sounded like the fall of a rotten tree, until the sound increased in frequency. Twenty-five seconds later, mortar rounds carpeted the canopy over our heads. Keeping an eye on the prisoner, I made a radio call for all personnel to rendezvous at a given location. I unwrapped the little guy and leading him by the cord worked my way through the pitch black jungle following my compass.

At the assembly site, I learned that five of the Cambodes were seriously injured by shrapnel. At dawn the enemy would be in hot pursuit of us and the box. To accomplish our mission, we would have to have a helicopter pick up the box and evacuate our wounded. Unfortunately, there were no known open areas in close proximity large enough to land a bird. Dropping a daisy cutter to blow an LZ would only give away our position. It was decided that a single chopper would use a jungle penetrator to secure the black box. A second ship would come in once we had identified a suitable LZ.

It all happened as planned. The box went out and we went on. At the first opening in the canopy large enough to accommodate a Huey, we circled our wagons and called in the medevac. The five wounded Cambodes were obvious with their tiger suits and M-16s. The VC was equally conspicuous with his Communist gear and light waxy features. As we were loading the Bodes, the crew chief inquired about the odorous sixth passenger. When I explained that he was a prisoner, the pilot radioed back that he would not allow him aboard. I stood on the left skid step by the aircraft commander's door. He shook his head pointing at the VC. I pulled out my Browning automatic and aimed it at the captive while yelling above the engine whine at the captain, 'This one's for you!'

Confused, he yelled back, 'What do you mean?'

I answered, 'If you do not take him, as soon as you pull pitch, I will shoot him in the head. You can come back here at any time and know a life was taken just for you!' I really had no intention of wasting the little guy. He was a hero. He had kept his part of the bargain and I would keep mine. I also knew Americans, and knew that the pilot, whose job was saving lives would not let regulations come before life. The little guy made the flight.

I had told the pilot to drop the VC wherever he delivered the Cambodes, and that is exactly what he did. When I went to visit my boys after clearing the war zone, I immediately saw three bright smiling Bodes with gold teeth. When I asked about the VC, the doc looked bewildered and replied, 'We received six WIAs identified as members of a special operations unit. We treated and released three of them; these you see had more serious wounds. I know nothing about an enemy casualty. We aren't allowed to treat enemy soldiers here. They are turned over to the Vietnamese.'

It's likely our hero made it past the ARVN guards, exiting the compound with American MPs. I've often wondered what happened to him. At least his wounds were tended to, he got a new uniform and a decent weapon. We recovered our technology. All in all it was in keeping with the holiday spirit.

One evening at the III Corps Officer's Club Bar, I overheard a second lieutenant from II Field Force Vietnam headquarters talking authoritatively about our black box mission and that we would soon be going into Zone C on an extended unconventional warfare operation. It was the break I was waiting for.

The next morning I informed Colonel Kelly of the security breach and recommended that we shift our operational area to War Zone D. We had already been to Duc Phuong and the enemy might think it was more of the same. Zone D was extremely mountainous, which would make encirclement much more difficult. Kelly got approval from Westmoreland. Out of the perfectly balanced 250-man guerrilla force only 100 stood in formation at the appointed day. Colonel Kelly was there for the send off. He looked downhearted reviewing the anaemic task force. It was the first time I had seen him look defeated, but it wouldn't be the last. He knew how hard we had tried, and the difficulty of the task before us. With sad resignation he concluded, 'Well, I guess we had better cancel Blackjack-31.'

'No Sir,' I said. 'We can still function as a mobile guerrilla force.' With that I evened off the three main-force platoons and the pathfinder and tail gunner teams of the recon. As it turned out, 250 would have been too many—100 was exactly right!

The mission was a total success. We had performed tactical miracles including the use of B-52 raids, sky-spot high altitude pinpoint bombing, river interdiction and crossings. (Most of the Bodes didn't swim.) After 30 days of living on the edge following elephant trails we were all ready for a shower and a hot meal. Kelly had said that we should plan to be in the field for 30 days. We were ready to come out. Then came more orders from SF headquarters: cross the Song Dong Nai River and continue operations to the north. The Bodes had had enough and revolted.

We had circled our wagons for a chow break when Jim Donahue, our medic, joined me. Jim was concerned that something was up. There was more talk than usual and a feeling of anxiety.

Fang, so nicknamed because of his massive lower jaw and incisor teeth, came over, snapped to attention, saluted, and revealed the problem: 'Captain Gritz, we know you want to have a big battle and kill all the Communist. We know how to do that. We will remain here for a few days and the enemy will all come for us. We will have a big battle, kill off the enemy, and then we can go home for Tet!'

No doubt, if we didn't keep moving, there would be a big battle. Tet, New Year, was an important holiday and a time of family gathering. I explained to Fang that it was not my choice, our orders were to continue.

'Sir, we fight hard for you. Now we must go home. We go no further!'

It was customary around midday for an Air Force Forward Air Controller to come up on the radio to see if we were still alive and in need of tactical air support. 'Smokey' had a flight of F-100s standing by.

I instructed Fang to inform the Cambodian chain of command that they had three choices: first, continue to follow my instructions; second, stack all the weapons and equipment in a large pile and go on their own; third, keep the equipment and become an enemy! The SF team would move out in 15 minutes with or without the Task Force. Jim Donahue was concerned that the Bodes would take us captive, but the thought hadn't entered my mind. With a mirror flash I made sure that the FAC had our position, and informed him of my current leadership problem—Cambodes in revolt. I asked for an after-burner low pass to be followed by 20 mm strafing runs on the flanks. The low pass convinced the Bodes to continue, for just one more week!

We had all pondered the 'choice-of-assignment' lure. I warned the team that due to the totally unexpected success of BJ-31, there would likely be a miniseries of Blackjacks. The men were adamant. If Westmoreland asked us to stay together for just one more mission impossible, they were going to sing him a hymn. The SF hymn was fairly straightforward, just two words: 'Hummmm, him him, fuck him!'

During the briefing, a staff intelligence colonel stood and made quite a speech about the value of enemy prisoners in building an intelligence estimate. He then noted that a number of POWs were taken and wondered where they were now? My comment was that they all died. We then had a brief exchange of *'They died?'* 'They died;' *'They died?'* 'They died;' *'They died . . . ?'* 'They died!' This was interrupted by Westmoreland, who called a break. He asked that I join him outside. Placing his arm around my shoulders, he said in a kindly way, 'Bo, you must be careful how you answer my staff. They don't have the insight to know what must be done when guerrilla forces have no way to secure, care for, or transport prisoners.'

I asked quietly, 'General, do you want me to lie to your staff?' 'No, I don't want you to lie. I just want you to be careful in your choice of words.' Westmoreland did ask us to stay together for just one more operation. I heard the team tuning up for the hymn, but instead they agreed to remain and return to the watering hole, knowing that one day the tiger would be waiting.

Based on our success, Westmoreland authorized two mobile guerrilla task forces to be formed in each corps area. As provisional units, we had no home base and so took up residence in a rubble pile outside of Trang Sup, the CIDG Training Center at Tay Ninh. I helped Captain Tom Johnson's MGTF-966 prepare for BJ-32, which turned out to be a routine long-range patrol operation. BJ-33, however, was much more dynamic. We were called upon to work jointly with Project Sigma under the operational control of the 1st US Infantry Division, then commanded by Major General John Hay. General Hay and his deputy, General Bernard Rogers, wanted us to find and fix a division-sized NVA force operating in an area between the Song Be and Song Dong Nai Rivers. My orders were to become decisively engaged so the enemy would mass and 'the Big Red One could jump on them!' It felt good knowing an American Infantry Division was right behind us. Our Pathfinders found the enemy on day three. As instructed, they circled up next to a large dry lake and prepared to fight, as the main force platoons raced to reinforce them.

It all worked exactly as planned—all except the part about

the Big Red One. We ended up in a tiny die-in-place perimeter firing from behind the stacked bodies of our dead and a large ant hill. The enemy's heavy machine guns, rockets, mortars, and artillery mowed down all the jungle cover around us from ranges beyond our light weapons. In the beginning, General Hay, aboard his command helicopter, said he was holding back his soldiers until the enemy massed sufficiently. At one time he asked me how we were doing. I replied that we had 50 per cent casualties. He asked if we could break out in small groups and attempt to reach Phuoc Vinh. I told him we would not leave our seriously wounded. An hour or so later, General Rogers was up. We were at a 75 per cent casualty rate. He informed me that none of the Big Red One would be deployed. He said that arrangements had been made for massive close air support and helicopter gunships. Just as the sun was about to set, we broke the back of the enemy encirclement having expended 100 sorties of TAC air and more than 100 sorties of armed helicopter gunfire. Empty lift-ships then came in to take us all to the Iron Cross Brigade headquarters at Phuoc Vinh. I was the last to leave the siege site. I picked up an MGTF-957 patch that had been shot off a uniform—we would leave nothing for the enemy.

I was met by General Hay and Blackjack Kelly. General Hay was most apologetic. 'Now, young fella, we didn't mean to leave you out there. No one could have known it was going to be that bad. I just couldn't put my Americans on the ground under those circumstances. General Westmoreland needs your situation report. How many of the enemy did you kill? What is your estimate of the number killed by air?'

He didn't like my answer. 'General, I don't know if we killed anyone. We were fighting from behind the bodies of our comrades. There wasn't time to count, only fight for our lives.'

Hay promptly turned to his G-3 ops chief and said, 'Tell COMUSMACV there were 400 confirmed killed by ground with another 400 probables, and 400 killed by air confirmed with 400 probable!"

I combined what was left of A-303 with 304 and MGTF 957 with 966. We left the next day for the Special Forces camp at Dong Xoai. The next two weeks were a running gun battle within the perimeter of an NVA division located just outside eight-inch Howitzer range of the 1st Infantry Division at Phuoc Vinh. In the end, we had all but equalled Hay's estimate to Westmoreland—and the Big Red One was able to administer the *coup de grâce*. We had just raided and attacked a regimental headquarters with fighter bombers. The enemy was chasing us out of their area toward Phuoc Vinh—and artillery range. At last, out maneuvered, cut off and encircled, I checked the map and called in a fire mission. Before it was over the 1st Infantry Division fired 4 000 rounds of eight-inch and 155 mm in forming a corridor of steel through which we moved until the enemy was forced to withdraw.

General Hay was aghast at the numbers of NVA so close to his own base. He asked me how we were able to travel so far without logistical support? He explained that his brigades required 150 000 pounds of food alone each day, making it impossible to venture out so far from established landing fields. I showed him our standard indigenous ration (we carried a week's worth of food in our rucksacks).

Upon examination Hay exclaimed, 'My God! These fish still have their eyes! How do they taste?'

'Sort of like popcorn, Sir.'

'Well, we could never feed Americans with this.'

'What do you think we are, Sir?'

'Well, you are Special Forces!'

I suddenly felt very good.

General Fred Weyand was a tall three-star from Texas with a soft reassuring manner. He commanded II Field Forces—half the troops in Vietnam. It was his idea to use the MGTF to gather intelligence, attack difficult targets, and perform a myriad of commando-type missions. I explained to him that the guerrilla forces were limited to two and a half miles per hour and worked best covering an area over an extended period of time. If we were to be on immediate call for high risk missions, we would need to reorganize and retrain. I explained the communication problem with the Bodes. I explained that often we took more fire from the rear than from the enemy. We would need cannon fodder. I requested volunteers from LBJ (Long Binh Jail). General Weyand countered that we could not send Americans on such dangerous missions. Instead, he agreed to furnish five long range recon personnel (LRRPs) on a continuous basis from each division within III and IV Corps. I knew the generals would send their riff-raff—exactly what I wanted. Only the Australians seemed concerned. I was called to their liaison office in Saigon. A lieutenant colonel asked me straight out what the chances were of his men coming back alive? I told him, 'Possibly as high as 50 per cent.' He thanked me for my honesty and said I would be receiving five of their finest—right!

I was promoted to Major and given command over both guerrilla A-Teams and their Cambodian forces, along with the 25 LRRPs, and a 500-man Chinese Nung 'Mike Force' with its own A-Team of SF. We were designated B-36. And so I'm here to introduce you to the making of some warriors to add to the select few who stand amongst the elite.

Stan Krasnoff tells his story as one of the B-36 men within this volume. Soldiers wear fancy uniforms, parade, and are put on display; warriors live in the shadows, study dirty tricks, and await impossible missions. Soldiers have careers and retirements being a warrior is a way of life. If you're intrigued, you should be! Read on.

James Bo Gritz

CONTENTS

ACKNOWLEDGEMENTS

I could not have written this story without the help of the Rapid Fire survivors whose pithy comments enliven this tale. In particular I owe much to Bernie Newman's diligence in running down after-action reports. Many others contributed even though some found it hard to walk that grim jungle path of three decades ago. Pete Stark, Saint Laurent, Jim Donahue, Richard Deo, Dave Morrison and Dave Spencer were just some of those. I thank Smokey Barnes for his expert advice on air operations. His words reflected the same professional attitude that had gained him great respect among the Rapid Fire troopers. I am grateful to Bo Gritz whose words lend perspective and power to this story.

This book is dedicated to all the members of Project Rapid Fire who trod that jungle path and stared into the baleful eye of the tiger.

ACRONYMS

AO	Area of Operations
ARVN	Army of the Republic of Vietnam
C&C	Command and control
CIDG	Citizens Indigenous Defence Group
COMUSMACV	Commander United States Military Assistance Command, Vietnam.
COSVN	Central Office for South Vietnam
DEROS	Date of estimated return from overseas
ELINT	Electronic Intelligence
FAC	Forward air control
FOB	Forward Operational Base
IO	Intelligence officer
KIA	Killed in action
LAW	Light anti-tank weapon
LRRP	Long Range Reconnaissance Patrol
LZ	Landing zone
MGF	Mobile Guerilla Force
MUST	Medical Unit Self Contained Transportable
NLF	National Liberation Front
NVA	North Vietnamese Army
RPG	Rocket-propelled grenade
SF	Special Forces
SOG	Special Operations Group
TOC	Tactical Operations Center
VC	Viet Cong

SOUTH VIETNAM: A GENERAL PERSPECTIVE

PROLOGUE

PROLOGUE

'What the hell are they waiting for?' the middle-aged man at the table two down from me says loudly. 'They're only a mob of goatherders.' The woman sitting next to the man casts an embarrassed glance at him as he riffles the pages of his paper to emphasise his point.

I sit at my favourite table in Sandy's Deli on Noosa's Hastings Street. It's one month since the September 11 terrorist attacks on the World Trade Center and the Pentagon and of course the man is referring to the war in Afghanistan, focusing specifically on the lack of ground forces' engagement of the Taliban by the Americans. I sip my cappuccino taking a moment to consider the comment that discomposed the man's companion. He's quite wrong of course, referring to the opposition as nothing but a mob of goatherders; I happen to know.

Let me explain. During the Soviet invasion of Afghanistan two American Special Forces men, Nestor Pino and Bo Gritz, were responsible for the training of the Mujahadeen. And of course the Mujahadeen formed part of the Taliban's land forces. All this happened with the imprimatur of the US Secretary of State for Security Assistance.

1

I remember my first meeting with Nestor Pino one afternoon back in late '67 at our base camp at Tay Ninh, Vietnam. He had emerged glassy-eyed and shell-shocked from his fortified camp of Tien Nghon, five kilometres to the north of us. At night from our base—regular as the nightly dumping of wet-season rain—we heard the rumble of enemy mortars as they pounded Captain Pino's sad little shithole in the jungle. Pino had served as an airborne company commander in the Cuban Brigade for the Bay of Pigs invasion before moving on to bigger and better things in Vietnam's War Zone C. At the time he was recruited, Pino was a regular Army colonel.

The other specialist was Bo Gritz, my Special Projects boss in Vietnam. Gritz came from the Bible Belt, steeped in a belief in God and the American Way. With patriotic fervour he set about selecting the array of weapons the Mujahadeen would need to bring them into the twentieth century, some of them with bizarre results. Gritz tells the story of how a project to modify one of the rotating barrels from an A-10 Warthog fighter plane, to be used as a weapon against Soviet tanks, went wrong. The program had gone up in smoke when the gun was brought into Washington for a demonstration. The A-10, which was in a covered truck, accidentally discharged on the main street, its projectile penetrating the vehicle and hitting a gasoline pump being used by a morning commuter. I can imagine the suits on Capitol Hill finding *that* one a tad difficult to explain to the harassed DC cops swarming the scene.

Anyhow, a remotely piloted system was organised to combat the huge rock-walled forts that were constructed by the Soviets. A radio-controlled 1000 pound bomb would be released at 25 000 feet and fly up to 50 miles, either homing in on a stationary beacon or hand-guided to the target by an observer. The Mujahadeen were also provided with the Barrett, a 50 calibre sniper rifle with a telescopic sight that can knock a person's head off at a range greater than two kilometres using armour-piercing explosive rounds. With this weapon the Mujahadeen guerillas interdicted bridges spanning the Russian/Afghan border as well as critical targets within Afghanistan. That's just some of the boys' toys to be added to the Stinger heat-seeking missile and a few others in the grab bag tossed to our Taliban goatherders, compliments of the Mujahadeen. But I'm getting ahead of myself.

The man with the newspaper and the angry words has another problem now. A middle-aged lady with frizzy salt-and-pepper hair has joined the debate. From her spot at the next table, she smiles benevolently and says, 'Pray for peace. There's nothing to be achieved by attacking the poor people of Afghanistan.' Well, this has really lit a fire. 'Peace! What about the 6000 dead in the World Trade Center and the Pentagon?' growls the man. His companion rolls her eyes, a martyred look of inevitability on her face. In a calm voice, Frizzy Hair puts in a couple of good shots about the need to educate rather than eradicate and the point about the lack of evidence linking the al-Qaida network with the terrorist attacks. 'Musharraf's a Muslim and he was satisfied with the evidence!' the man rejoins.

I cast a quick glance at our man, impressed by his counter thrust. He is referring to General Musharraf of Pakistan, who walks a tightrope in his own country as a result of his stance. My eyes drift to the newspaper hastily discarded. Part of the folded page shows a photograph of two Taliban leaders— sombre dark faces shrouded in black. The caption reads: TALIBAN WILLING TO DIE FOR JIHAD. I had recently read a comment made by the dashing General Patton, made famous during World War II: *I want you to remember that no bastard ever won a war by dying for his country. He won it by making the other poor dumb bastard die for his country.* That pretty well encapsulates the widely differing approaches. I'm almost persuaded to join in the debate. I have information about what's happening and could contribute, but finally am disinclined to do so. The man is too loud and Frizzy Hair is a simpering do-gooder who sets my teeth on edge.

I sigh. What gets to me more than anything is the evil in human beings. I live in a beautiful place girded by lakes and headlands jutting into the sea. Lush pastoral land blends with coastal heath to form an idyllic setting for peace and tranquillity, yet my thoughts have been disrupted by the news of weapons-grade anthrax and the ease with which chemicals can be obtained to develop nerve agents that will kill thousands of innocent people. And what's more, the madmen who may procure these would not even be in breach of the *Controlled Substances Act*!

There's little doubt that terrorism, given the type of weapons available today, poses a threat to civilisation. But, pardon my cynicism, not everything is as it meets the eye. Did you know that at the height of the Vietnam War the port of Haiphong, which was a massive dump of enemy war matériel, was never bombed by the Americans? Why? Because Rockefeller's Exxon oil refinery was in that seaport. Did you know that just before Saddam Hussein invaded Kuwait he was told by Ms April Glaspie, US Ambassador to Iraq, that America had no opinion on Iraq's border dispute with Kuwait? Could she have been *that* ill-informed? And whatever happened to the 800 tons of gold plundered by Saddam Hussein out of Kuwait? Am I stretching the long bow if I suggest that maybe the booty was his pay-off for being the fall-guy? But I'm digressing.

So, back to the subject of the trio's vituperation; my sources tell me that once Mazar-i-Sharif falls to the Northern Alliance, the Taliban will be thrown out of power within seven to ten days and the real battle to locate and destroy the al-Qaida terrorist network will begin. And this brings me to the crux of my story: Rapid Fire.

You know, the thing about Rapid Fire was its 'in your face' approach—find the enemy and lock him into a close embrace (there's just a hint of sexual connotation to that statement which was definitely missing in War Zone C all those years ago). 'Beat the brushes and see what you can spook up,' Bo used to say with a sardonic little grin that usually meant yet another episode of adrenalin-pumping, heart-yammering, knock-down-drag-out madness.

While Special Forces in general have long carried out behind-the-lines reconnaissance tasks, Project Rapid Fire was unique. Born of desperation in a time of confusion and uncertainty, Rapid Fire is as relevant today as it was 30 years ago. Something gives me the feeling that the Special Forces troopers in Afghanistan are going to be nothing more than glorified forward air controllers directing bombs on the ground on behalf of the Northern Alliance. If that's the case, then you can kiss Bin Laden goodbye—he will simply slip across the unprotected Pakistani border. However, Rapid Fire tactics would use independent action to smoke out the bear, then corral him.

But there I go, getting ahead of myself again. So instead, dear reader, let me take you down the path of my story. Come back in time with me, to the jungles and cities of wartime Vietnam.

1 FLICKERING SHADOWS

Up close and personal. The image of the enemy's face screamed at me in my sleep. He was riding his bike towards me. The brim of his pith helmet threw an oval shadow over his eyes, a bizarre dark knight coming at me from some mysterious medieval forest. At fifteen feet and closing, I could see the beads of sweat on his upper lip. Senses reeling, I darted a glance at the clacker that sat inches away from my right hand, close to the buttress of a fallen tree behind which I was lying. The clacker was connected to the claymore mine I had set up close to the track.

We had infiltrated at first light, four helicopters each carrying five men, and two empty slicks racing at treetop level to fool the enemy into believing that none of the choppers had touched down. At first, ominous silence with only the blood walloping in my eardrums—had they seen us? And then there was momentary relief as the spider monkeys took up their querulous screeching in the high canopy.

It was hot in the jungle, I must have dozed momentarily, but now with a rush of adrenalin and my heart hammering, it dawned on me that this was it. If I didn't do something—and damned quickly at that—our patrol would be spotted with the enemy literally on top of us. Frantically, I cut a glance ten feet to my right where Sonny Edwards lay prone, sharing the buttress where I was hiding. His head was nodding, eyes shut in a sluggish state of half-sleep, a rill of sweat running down into his soaked camouflage shirt at the V of the neck. As I held my breath, fully expecting the bicyclist to run right over the top of me, I realised that he had turned and I was now staring at a sweat-soaked back and a rucksack slung over spare shoulders. The track formed a hairpin bend around the protruding roots of the buttress Sonny and I were hiding behind. I had glimpsed it when I had crawled forward to set up my claymore. As the bike changed direction, I could see the enemy's right hand resting on the pistol grip of an AK-47 that was cradled against the steel frame of the bike, barrel downwards. The rider disappeared out of view behind a bush just as another took his place. This one had his pith helmet off, suspended by a strap just below his Adam's apple. And it was this one's face that has etched itself into my mind, the face that has haunted my subconscious for over 35 years. His black hair hung in untidy rats' tails covering his forehead and his skin was sallow, pulled tightly over hollow cheeks. His dark eyes seemed to be staring straight at me as he negotiated his bike around the bend in the track.

Whatever happened to left security? I thought frantically. We'd formed an ambush roughly in line with the fallen tree covering the heavily used track in a shallow U with the two flank security groups, each of two men, forming its stems. The idea was that one flank would spot the approaching enemy first and ascertain whether our ten-man patrol could handle the situation. To break squelch twice on the ANPRC-25 radio held at each flank meant that the target was vulnerable, multiple squelch breaks meant the enemy group was too large and if I activated the ambush we'd be in a world of shit. The dilemma was that I'd received no prior warning, so what to do? My greatest concern was that the enemy would spot us at any moment. After all, the hairpin bend was closer than Sonny dozing only a few feet away. Another problem was that the clacker to the second claymore covering the killing ground was next to him. In a hurry to set up, knowing the track was constantly in use, I'd neglected to run the wire from Sonny's claymore to my location, so I couldn't set off both claymores simultaneously.

I gritted my teeth and pressed my clacker just as the third bike rider hove into view, hoping to Christ that Sonny's reaction would be quick. There was an ear-shattering detonation and out of the corner of my eye I saw Sonny's head snap back as he was jolted into wakefulness. To my relief he squeezed his clacker in a reflex action and the second claymore detonated in a cloud of dust and whining shrapnel. Mouth dry and pulse hammering in my throat, I let go a full magazine from my rifle, which had been resting next to the clacker, pleased with the way the one-in-five tracer, on automatic, zipped low along the track towards where I thought the first bike rider would have been. The spent cartridges tinkled as they fell in a smoking heap beside the buttress. And then the rattle and pop spread like a raging bushfire with the patrol's M-16s opening up, a timpani of sound as more and more weapons joined in. After a few minutes I yelled 'cease fire' at the top of my lungs, reasonably confident that there was no sound of returning enemy fire. The roar abated, dissolving into single shots fired at random, and finally there was an eerie silence. I crawled out onto the track with my radio man on my heels, the flexi-cord of the ANPRC-25 set yoyoing as we dragged through the torn foliage, the radio's handpiece clipped to my webbing.

Through the haze of gun smoke I could see the slowly spinning wheel of a bicycle and, lying beside it, the upper torso of the enemy soldier who I'm sure had looked me in the eye only a few minutes earlier. Strangely, his expression had not changed even though the bottom half of his body had been shredded and the remnants of his khaki uniform were soaked with blood; the rest of him was dripping from the nearby trees. The shafts of sunlight breaking through the jungle canopy back-lit the smoke that hung in tatters on the jungle floor. Further down the track I could see Sonny checking out the other body, two other members of the patrol keeping watch as he rifled through the pockets of the dead man. Here I was, riveted to the spot, staring at the face of my enemy, whose dark eyes were now glazing over. Strangely, his face was not disfigured by the steel ball bearings that were released from the exploding claymore mine. We had to hurry. The Cambodian border was less than a stone's throw away, this was enemy territory and we would soon be hunted.

The legacies of my involvement have been the nightmares, nightmares that have persisted for over 35 years. Although I've had other operational experiences, both prior to and after the face on the bicycle, my nightmares always centred around that face.

Last night had been a moonlit night, a calm tranquil setting for a good night's rest, but I had woken up in the early hours, mouth dry, heart pumping with the drilling scream of fear ricocheting in my mind. I knew instantly that the scream had stopped short of my vocal chords. Shirley's measured breathing as she lay beside me attested to that. In the wan light of the moon, partially hidden by the fronds of a rhapis lady palm outside my bedroom, was the face. While I had slept, it had been stalking me, dark eyes mocking my indiscretion. It was late—probably too late—but I had to try. I had to get to him before . . . Inch by inch I lifted the bedclothes and slowly slipped from the bed. I could taste the salt of my sweat in the corners of my mouth as I glanced at the shadows of the palm on the bedroom wall. The face was clearly silhouetted there, a proof of its presence.

'What's wrong? Are you alright?' I heard my wife ask.

A bedside light clicked on and I was aware of being prone on the carpet, suddenly feeling ridiculous, exposed, embarrassed.

I've been married to Shirley for 35 years so I guess she knows pretty much all there is to know about my episodes, which gives me no satisfaction. I wouldn't wish those nightmares on my worst enemy, let alone someone I love. But I'm proud of the fact that my wife and I have celebrated our 35th anniversary. These days that's some kind of a record. It hasn't all been beer and skittles and we've had to work at it, but I'm old-fashioned enough to believe that if you take an oath before God then you should stick by it. Not that I'm religious. In fact I believe that Christianity is a great con job perpetrated by a conclave of clerics who wanted to gain power back in 100 or so AD. But I'm digressing; the point is, I believe there *is* a God, an omniscient being, and I *did* take an oath before Him.

Besides, I love my wife. I met Shirley in 1964 during my tour of duty with the Pacific Islands Regiment. She was a nurse at the Wewak Blood Bank and I was completing my second tour of outstation duty in New Guinea. I had never met a person with such an outgoing bubbly personality, who brought sunshine into the lives of so many people. The natives adored her and respected her professionalism, and the medical staff admired her tenacity. She had the unenviable task of getting villagers of the Sepik District to donate blood for the Wewak hospital, and that meant flying into some really hairy mountainous places that were often shrouded in fog for days.

My favourite watering hole outside of the officers' mess at Moem was the Sepik Club. I'd spend many of my off-duty hours at the club drinking beer and debating the virtues of rugby luminaries like Kenny Catchpole and Jules Guerassimoff with the plantation managers and civil servants who frequented the place. It was an important part of my leisure time and I treasured it, but eventually I stopped frequenting the club and my visits to the mess were limited to meals and official functions. It must have been love, that I would sacrifice so much just to sit and hold hands and talk the talk that women like: children, families and clothes.

This morning I felt a need to walk alone on the beach. I needed time and the right environment to try to rationalise why my nightmare had returned. After all, it was well over five years since the last visitation. Why had the face come back to haunt me? I have no recriminations and feel no remorse. In fact I'm proud to have been part of a highly trained professional group put into a tough situation. There were certain things we had to do. Whenever we pulled out we left one or two M-14 mines on the track—standard operating procedure—'toe poppers' we called them. The M-14 was a little plastic mine only two inches in diameter, about the size of a large pill bottle, that was activated by a pressure-release spring. More often than not the toe popper was the difference between escape and capture, delaying the enemy who inevitably pursued us with overwhelming force. We used instantaneous grenades too. It was easy to make them: just unscrew the striker mechanism out of the standard M-26 grenade, cut the detonator with a set of crimping pliers, dig the green timing paste out of the striker well and re-crimp the detonator—simple.

Brutal? Barbaric? Sure, but it's different when you're out there in tiger country and the tiger looks you squarely in the eye and you know that all he wants to do is tear you to pieces. I've seen what the enemy did to our own people, and it wasn't a pretty sight. There's been talk lately of banning the use of mines. Can you imagine in a future conflict an Australian unit dug-in on a hill somewhere, being told that its government is not prepared to fully provide for its protection? What do you say to the mothers, fathers, brothers and wives of those soldiers when that unit is overrun as a result of there being no anti-tank or anti-personnel mines to protect the perimeter? The problem is war itself, not the wherewithal that's necessary to prosecute it, and I can't imagine any Defence Force chief agreeing to such a policy.

The other thing to remember is that the soldier simply does the government's bidding. We kind of forgot that 30 years ago when it was the soldier's homecoming from Vietnam. Many Australians responded by hurling abuse at him as he stepped on his home soil. I clearly remember the instructions as my Qantas flight prepared to descend into Sydney. 'Make sure you don't wear your uniform, and don't talk about Vietnam while you're at Mascot.' The thing that really pissed me off was being classified as a 'child killer'. You know, it takes about three pounds to the square inch of pressure to squeeze off a shot from an AK-47. Any kid can do it and providing he's accurate that bullet will kill a person just as well as if it was fired by a 'hard-core' guerilla. And there were a lot of those kids hell-bent on wasting a US imperialist dog or one or two of his lackeys. What really gets to me is that three decades later we're happy to nonchalantly watch the morning news on TV, riveted by technicolour pictures of the previous night's road-kill or zoom shots of a murder victim sprawled grotesquely on the pavement while we shovel in Coco Pops or whatever else we eat for breakfast.

I sighed. My favourite beach walk is from Laguna Bay to the groyne at the mouth of the Noosa River, and this morning the tide was out and there was plenty of beach to walk on. As my feet squelched in the wet sand, I thought about how adversarial we humans are, and an old Spanish proverb popped into my mind: Before starting a vendetta, dig two graves. Anyhow it was pleasant walking this time of the morning, sharing my beach with two strangers and a lone oyster-eater scurrying back and forth in the wash searching for shellfish. A cool south-easter helped my mood and by the time I reached the boardwalk on the way back I had come to the conclusion that I should revisit that cauldron of Southeast Asia, if only in my mind, in the hope of allaying the ghosts. I felt better and decided to indulge myself with a cappuccino. I chose a secluded table around the back of Sandy's Delicatessen and settled to the pleasant task of browsing through the newspaper. Preoccupied with my own thoughts I was only vaguely aware that the table two down from me had been occupied.

I was distracted by the voice of a child about six or seven years old. The kid's features came into view as I lowered my newspaper. He looked a tough little bastard with a mop of hair crowned by a baseball cap with its peak reversed. Pizza crumbs rimmed his mouth and he had that defiant look so common amongst kids these days. He was grumbling at his mother. She was in her early twenties, which would have made her about sixteen when she conceived. She had three rings in her left ear, one in her left nostril and one through her belly button that showed from beneath a short top. She was talking with a bloke called Simon. I focused half-heartedly on what she was saying. Yackety-yack this and that . . . 'That was a filthy party last night?' I winced at her slovenly speech and the mindlessness of her topic.

I thought of Nina, my grandmother, and was struck by how the world had changed. Nina would have had washerwoman's hands at the same age as this . . . this bird. I sighed, the pang of guilt catching me in my throat. Nina used to do the work of two men. She'd carry the week's shopping in two bulging string bags, her arms straining as she dragged her feet up the steep hill to the house we lived in. There were no supermarkets in 1950 and Nina used to walk down to the Camp Hill terminus at tram stop 33, nearly a mile away, to shop at the local grocery store. This was after she'd done the washing, wrestling over a steam copper in the basement of the rented house.

The young mother was still quacking on, ending declarative

sentences with a question. What the hell's happened to education? She was bemoaning her fate, having recently been dumped by somebody called Chad. So it would seem that the kid was probably not the offspring of Simon, but possibly of Chad. A little annoyed at being sidetracked, I tried to return to my original train of thought which centered around a bunch of people I had last seen three decades ago: Bernie Newman, the Hulk, Bo Gritz and the rest of them, all members of Rapid Fire. Just the thought of Rapid Fire sent shivers up and down my back. I hadn't thought much about Vietnam over the years. But now that I'd started, I had to press on—cross the Rubicon.

2 EYES AND EARS

From Cholon and the squalor of Sampan Alley to the gracious tree-lined boulevards, Saigon reflected the doubts and uncertainties of a troubled city. I remember in '67 the confusion I had about the population. Looking at the sea of faces on the teeming streets I'd wondered what the people thought of us, puzzled by the expressions of dislike and even animosity shown by some.

Years later I remember a conversation I had on this subject with a Vietnamese expatriate now living in one of the western suburbs of Sydney. Nguyen had been an interpreter for the First Australian Task Force at Nui Dat in Phuoc Tuy province and had escaped just before the fall of Saigon in '75. 'What do you expect?' he'd said. 'The Americans gave us inflation and in return took our wives and daughters.' Now I don't know that that's altogether a fair comment, nor do I know whether this attitude contributed to the scarcity of intelligence through the South Vietnamese channels, but there was a dearth of information. To compound the problem, intelligence agencies were short of funds to pay informers and this left a void that so troubled . . . hell, I'd forgotten the name of the general who was the commander of the field force—Two Field Force Victor

15

we called it. Anyhow, I could picture the bloke, but not put a name to him . . . old age creeping up.

Weyand! That's it. The general's name was Weyand and he was getting a lot of ELINT that seemed to point to an invasion of South Vietnam by the North Vietnamese Army (NVA). ELINT is short for electronic intelligence. You know, stuff like infrared imaging, sideways-looking aerial radar and 'people sniffers'—aircraft-mounted sensors capable of detecting large volumes of ammonia in the jungle. Anyhow, ELINT indicated enemy troop movements from north to south along the border areas. The idea seemed ludicrous since the enemy was being beaten in the 'brushfire' battles that raged throughout South Vietnam.

About this time Weyand lost Project Omega, a major strategic intelligence unit, to General Westmoreland who was the overall commander of the Military Assistance Command–Vietnam, or Macvee as it was called.

Omega had been formed in October '66 with its command post at Ban Me Thuot and four roadrunner teams, later increased to eight, deployed under operational command of Two Field Force Victor. Sixteen recon teams with some Australian SAS troopers provided the eyes for the unit. The roadrunner teams, manned by indigenous personnel of Vietnamese ethnicity, dressed like the Viet Cong and were tasked with infiltrating local enemy units—an unenviable task to say the least! Montagnards of the Sedang, Jeh and Rhade tribes provided the brunt of the recon element. I don't know much about Omega, but it seems to me that working with the hotchpotch of ethnic groupings would have been like sitting on a powder keg for the hundred or so American Special Forces and the few SAS attached to them.

Anyhow, the loss of Omega shaped Weyand's requirements. He needed a unit with a long-range special reconnaissance capability able to provide immediate information on the enemy anywhere in Vietnam. To do this in the shortest of time frames, the unit had to be able to capture prisoners and track enemy units. Weyand turned to the only person at the time who had the experience to get the job done. He called on James 'Bo' Gritz. At the time Gritz was in command of the Mobile Guerilla Force (MGF), a unique outfit if ever there was one. Ten American Special Forces personnel and some 250 Cambodians put together to sneak around in the enemy's backyard. No other unit in Vietnam had successfully operated in enemy-held territory as a guerilla force.

The mention of Cambodians these days conjures up thoughts of the Khmer Rouge. The Cambodians of the MGF, however, were politically the opposite of the Khmer Rouge. The Khmer Serei or soldiers of the Free Cambodia Movement were mostly recruited from a Special Forces camp at Bu Dop, north-west of Bien Hoa, although by the latter stages of 1967 this means had nearly dried up and more and more recruits were coming from Cao Lanh near Saigon. Being border people who lived much of their time in Vietnam, the Khmer Serei had been drafted by the South Vietnamese government into the Citizens Indigenous Defence Group (CIDG), or 'Sidge'. The Khmer Serei were a truly remarkable people. Taller and physically stronger than the Vietnamese, they had to make their way in a society that considered them to be of a lower class and this caused tension between the two groups. Proudly independent, with a hatred of communism, the Khmer Serei were ideal recruits for the MGF.

At the time that Gritz was being briefed by Weyand, the MGF had just completed two operations, the first of which was to locate and retrieve the black box from a downed U2 reconnaissance plane in enemy-occupied territory. The second, in late '66, had been in War Zone C where the force had successfully held out in enemy-held territory for 60 days, disrupting their supply route. The unit had taken casualties and was in the process of refitting. To do Weyand's bidding, Gritz had to restructure the MGF so that instead of melting into the jungle on contact, it could hold ground taking advantage of added firepower, but still retain the ability of being airlifted quickly when the enemy concentrated large numbers against it. That's how Project Rapid Fire came into being in July '67 when the new provisional unit, B-36, replaced the MGF.

While Bu Dop and Cao Lanh provided Cambodian reinforcements for the new provisional unit, I could imagine the manning problems Gritz would have had in filling the officer and senior NCO cadre. The US army would hardly have tripped over itself in a hurry to produce its best people for what could only be described as a suicide mission. I've spent 22 years in the Australian army and in that time I've met more than my fair share of 'wannabes'. Which reminds me of the time my battalion was at Woodside in South Australia. It was 1980 and we were about to conduct a live-fire and movement exercise at the back of a place called Leigh Creek on the verge of the South Australian desert. Under pressure from the brigade commander, I had invited the local militia commander to participate with some of his troops. The night before the exercise was to start my mess had a dining-in night and the militia commander was invited. Throughout the evening he regaled us with stories of his men's expertise and his own depth of knowledge in all training matters. Frankly, the man was a bloody bore and after a while his loud voice started to grate. Though I'm not fond of the trappings of social etiquette, I enjoy a good dining-in night surrounded by men whose common interests lend the warmth of camaraderie to the table. The fine wine too, is very pleasant, but this bloke put a dampener on the evening. My adjutant was too polite to pick him up on some of his more outlandish comments and I was frankly too tired to bother. The next morning he and his men duly paraded for the exercise. My RSM wisely split his people amongst the battalion's rifle companies to help them out. I led off in the centre of the forward platoon of the first company with my guest by my side. With mortars dropping live rounds 300 yards to our flank, the platoon moved off. We were practising a technique called 'pepper potting' that required the front line to be numbered. All odd numbers would fire while the even numbers rushed forward a few steps, then dropped to the ground and commenced firing while the odd numbers rushed up to the line, and so the technique was repeated. We had progressed a short distance when I noticed the marked absence of my guest. Turning around, I found him skulking behind an old mallee root. The man had simply frozen and no amount of encouragement could prise him away from his mallee root. You know, some people talk a lot of nonsense about courage in action. As far as I'm concerned it's all about how an individual overcomes fear. Fear is the natural reaction of a sane person put into a life-threatening situation, and how he grapples with this fear to perform his duty is the true measure of courage.

So I could envision the problems confronting Gritz. He would have been inundated with people who sounded fine in barracks, especially when fortified by booze, but who were unable to handle constant close-quarter contact with the enemy. He would have had to cull them quickly. Inevitably he would have fallen back on the 'hard cases'—the army establishment cast-offs. I think secretly he probably relished the challenge, sensing an affinity with those rejected free spirits who questioned orthodoxy and flew in the face of tradition. Like a hard-bitten mongrel dog, B-36 grew out of that tough no-nonsense environment its predecessor had provided. The hard-core members simply called it Task Force.

I served in B-36, and my memories of it are as vivid now as they were all those years ago. Fate joined three Australians and a handful of Yanks for a wild ride that forged a brotherhood never to be broken. In retrospect I'd always thought it was strange that Australians were involved, seeing that the brunt of Rapid Fire operations was on the Cambodian border where no

Aussie troops ventured, but I suppose it was a measure of US respect for the professionalism of our troops. I was excited at the thought of revisiting that part of the past that invoked in me both the feeling of exhilaration and bone-chilling terror. We'd had a lot of laughs too.

3

BLUNDERING TOWARDS RAPID FIRE

Looking back on it, the first step I had taken towards becoming a candidate for Rapid Fire was an inadvertent one. It came during my first tour of duty at the Jungle Training Centre, Canungra. I'd been sent there in '66 as a captain in charge of battle efficiency training for soldiers posted to Vietnam. Part of my job required me to conduct grenade practices that were carried out at a place called Back Creek, just behind the ridges of Battle Wing. One day we had just completed grenade throwing with a bunch of students when the senior sergeant on my team sidled up to me. 'Have you ever played spot-the-flash, Skip?' Chris Pope asked. I hadn't played any such game and said so. 'How about we have a go?' Pope went on, his eyes cutting to Dave Wallner, a fellow instructor and off-duty drinking mate of his. 'Let's do it, boss, we've got a few grenades to spare,' urged Wallner. Conducting a grenade practice is one of the most boring activities you can think of, so it was partly to break the monotony and boredom of the past few hours that I agreed to give it a go. And so we'd gone out in front of the sandbagged throwing bays, three sergeants carrying a partly filled box of M-26 grenades, and a bemused junior captain.

Just clear of the impact area with its blasted soil, Pope called a halt. 'The game's real simple,' he said. Leaning over the box he selected a fully primed grenade. 'All you got to do is pull the pin and throw the damn thing as far as you can.' I'll explain to the uninitiated. An orthodox grenade practice involves rolling a grenade over-arm and then ducking behind a wall of sandbags for cover. 'Throwing the damn thing' in this case meant standing out in the open, bereft of all cover. And that's just what Pope did, letting the lever that holds the firing pin go in the process. I stood dumbstruck as the lever bounced off my chest and fell at my feet while the grenade spiralled end over end in the cloudless afternoon sky. I held my breath. There was indeed a star-shaped red flash that was followed by the crack of the exploding grenade downhill from where we stood, a distance of twenty yards or so. 'Did you spot the flash, Skipper?' Pope grinned. All four of us had remained standing in the open and I can tell you that first grenade going off fairly makes your ring pucker. We spent the best part of half an hour then, throwing grenades, finishing up with a crescendo as all four of us let fly at the trees.

Back at Battle Wing we replaced stores and as I was preparing to head for home, residual adrenalin still in my veins, I was confronted by the wing adjutant. 'The colonel wants to see you right away!' The adjutant of course was referring to the Chief Instructor of Battle Wing, Lieutenant Colonel Mann. Joe Mann was a legend in the army. A veteran of World War II where he'd been given command of a company as a subaltern at Gona during the New Guinea campaign, he was also in the thick of it in Korea. Joe stood six feet in his socks and weighed all of 250 pounds. He had arms the size of an average person's thighs and shoulders that would barely fit through a barn door, and when I saw him glowering at me from behind his desk what little courage I had flew out the window.

'What the hell's going on out there?' Joe snapped.

'Where, Sir?' I asked, immediately sorry for the banality.

'Back bloody Creek, that's where!' Joe raised himself on the knuckles of his hands. 'I've been sitting here listening to the sounds of a grenade practice going on all day. Crump . . . crump . . . crump. Predictable . . . every couple of minutes. And then all of a sudden it's like D-Day out there!' Joe pointed a spatulate finger at me. 'I know what you and your bloody sergeants were doing out there. You bastards were playing spot-the-flash!' Joe was slavering at the mouth. 'If I ever catch you doing that again I'll kick your arse!' he roared.

As I exited hurriedly I thought I detected a gleam in Joe's eye, but I wasn't going to hang around to find out. I think he'd misunderstood my ignorance for bravado and somewhere in his notebook he might have pencilled a note to the effect that if ever an opportunity arose where normal troops could be spared my presence, it should be taken up. Give the monkey a cage. I feel that was my first step towards Rapid Fire.

I'd only just settled in to thinking about old times when the kid once again interrupted. He's off between the tables, baggy pants and Nike joggers disappearing into the gents toilet. In his haste he'd tripped over my outstretched legs. 'Ashley,' the mother called out and looked to Simon for help.

'Come back here, you little bastard,' Simon muttered half-heartedly, looking a bit embarrassed. I have some sympathy for young Ashley, who didn't ask to be brought into this world but who finds himself part of an extended family that doesn't seem to give a shit about him. He's probably got a rocky road ahead of him. I might be unduly pessimistic but I know what it's like to be displaced: I've spent nine months in a refugee camp on the island of Tubabao in the Philippines. I was born in Shanghai and my parents escaped from China in '49 when the communists took over. I was ten when I finished up in the Philippines as a refugee. Needless to say my memories of Shanghai are dimmed by time and distorted by a child's perspective. However, I can remember two huge bronze lions set on pedestals at the entrance to the Shanghai National Bank. The mildewed lions guarded a wide stairway leading to the bank. Actually, not all parts of the statues were mildewed. Pop once told me that to pat the lion's balls was supposed to bring good luck, and over time thousands of people had patted those bronze gonads as they walked past, leaving them as bright as the day they were cast.

Despite my pessimism about Ashley's chances I'm a firm believer in fate taking a hand in the game of life, sometimes sweetening the pot as it were. After all, it happened to me. When an old rust bucket called the *Krystobal* landed my family on Tubabao we were allotted to the fourth raiyon (district). In the slush and rain we were shown to a World War II army surplus tent that was just like all the other miserable refugees' tents on the island except that ours leaked a lot more than anybody else's. At least I thought so. However, one thing we were blessed with in the fourth raiyon was Uri's presence.

Uri was in his late twenties, but to us kids he was truly a wise old man. He had few friends and at the time we thought that was because of his strange ways, but in retrospect I suppose it was because he fell between two generations. All of Pop's cronies had fought in the civil war but Uri was just a baby then. The kids from the *Krystobal*, aged between ten and fourteen, were all too young for him, so Uri overcame his boredom by becoming our scoutmaster. It wasn't so much that he was a great scout leader that made him popular with us, in fact he hardly spoke to us, but what we all remember him for was his invention. Uri had crafted the most beautiful staple gun ever, and he brought it along to one of our scout meetings.

The meeting was held on the edge of a steep gully that separated the third raiyon from the fourth. We were all wary because the kids from the third were the meanest and toughest of all. They dominated the gully, peppering us with rocks. Actually I think they were just older and therefore rougher. Anyway, to walk through the gully was to tempt fate and many of us fourth raiyon kids ended up with bloodied heads.

That was until Uri introduced us to his invention. Uri's staple gun consisted of a piece of wood shaped into the butt and stock of a rifle with straps of car tubing fastened to it. Released by a hinged peg, the stretched rubber strap could send a fence staple flying up to 40 yards and the notched foresight made the gun amazingly accurate at that range. Once Uri's invention was mass-produced and passed out amongst us fourth raiyon kids the balance of power was tilted in our favour. We wreaked such havoc with our new weapon that two of the third raiyon kids had to be taken to hospital on Samar island with staples embedded in their flesh. Uri unfortunately lost his job as our scoutmaster, but I felt we had served our apprenticeship well under his guidance.

But while fate can throw up options to even things up as we proceed through life, it can also play nasty tricks. In early '67 I volunteered for service with a crack unit called the Australian Army Training Team to Vietnam, or the Team. In May '62 Colonel Ted Serong had taken the first contingent of 30 military instructors into Vietnam to instruct the South Vietnamese in jungle warfare, village defence and related engineering and signals activities. Since then the Team, which became one of the most highly decorated units in the history of the Australian Army, had provided officers and senior NCOs ostensibly for training purposes on attachment to the Army of the Republic of Vietnam or its militia equivalent, the Regional and Popular Forces or 'ruff puffs' as they were irreverently called. I say ostensibly because many of the 'teeth arms' members of the Team—infantry, armour and engineers— finished up in the Mobile Strike Force, or 'Mike Force', as a ready reaction to the numerous fortified camps deployed by the American Special Forces throughout South Vietnam. In fact I was told that I was earmarked to join a Mike Force unit. I was also told that I would have Christmas at home and be posted early in the New Year. With that in mind I was looking forward to enjoying the festive season, my second as a married man, at Canungra. And that's where fate stepped in.

Tragically, in late '67 a good friend and fellow captain, Karl Baudistel, was killed in action just out of Da Nang and my posting was brought forward. In Saigon I was told that I was no longer going to Mike Force, but was off instead to a Special Projects unit. What unit? The question was met by a blank expression and some bureau-babble that made little sense other than the fact that there were two other Aussies involved, Sonny Edwards, a roly-poly red-faced little bloke who had flown from Australia with me, and Jim Cahill, both newly promoted SAS warrant officers. Cahill had been 'in-country' for four months and was in the hospital at Nui Dat suffering from amoebic dysentery.

So that's how I found myself in the back of a staff car on the road from Saigon to Bien Hoa in the company of the Team's commanding officer. We were being driven at breakneck speed and as we whipped past a long convoy of military trucks I asked the driver, out of curiosity, why he was going so fast. 'To avoid ambush, Sir,' the driver responded, casting an incredulous glance at me. I think I'd have preferred to take my chances with an ambush rather than the possibility of dying in a flaming car wreck on the side of the Saigon–Bien Hoa Highway. Anyway, I felt deflated, particularly with the driver's comment coming on the heels of the disquieting conversation I'd just had with the Team's commanding officer in the back seat. 'The commander of the group you're joining is a bloke called Gritz, Major Gritz. He's a bit gung-ho so keep your head down.'

That was all? I had no idea of what Gritz did or where he was. To bolster my sagging spirits I entertained the thought that perhaps I was to be enlightened at the headquarters of Special Forces Company A in Bien Hoa where we were heading. But this was not to be. The Team's CO bade Sonny Edwards and me a hurried farewell as we jumped aboard an Iroquois helicopter that took us to Tay Ninh. Sonny had done his National Service in '58 and loved it so much that he had enlisted full-time. His wife Thelma had pined for her hometown of Perth so much that Sonny joined the SAS Regiment to get her home.

He was in Sydney when his posting to Vietnam had come through and now he looked just as nonplussed as I, his fair-complexioned face growing mottled in the melting heat.

Many years later, reading Gritz's book *Called To Serve*, I came upon a section that dealt with the Aussie CO who had asked him what the chances of survival were for the Aussies about to join B-36. Gritz had said 'fifty-fifty'. I can now understand the inadequate briefing, which was probably due to the fact that nobody apart from Weyand and Gritz knew much about Rapid Fire. But I think Sonny Edwards and I deserved to know our chances. That still rankles. I recently heard that Sonny died of a heart attack in '84. The news of his death saddens me. 'Sounds like a lulu of an outfit,' Sonny had growled, rolling his eyes as we were about to take off for Tay Ninh.

Tay Ninh is close to the Cambodian border, north-west of Saigon and on the edge of War Zone C, a huge area of secondary jungle with bamboo-choked waterways. The helicopter landed us there in the early afternoon. The city is a sprawl of single-storeyed white stucco buildings with thatched nipa palm roofs that spilled almost onto the runway of the airstrip. On the other side of the tarmac, pitched among the rubber trees of a plantation, was an untidy group of army tents. In the few years since graduating from Officer Cadet School I'd gained a name for being unconventional, and I thought I'd become inured to most things, but what confronted me as I moved in the direction of the rubber trees simply blew me away.

As I walked in the heat of a dry season afternoon with the smell of nuoc mam—fish sauce—and ripe tropical fruit wafting across the tarmac, I was overcome by a feeling of unreality. It was as if I had stepped onto a movie set depicting some camp run by crazy revolutionaries. There were men moving in and out of a tent marked TOC—Tactical Operations Center. They wore camouflage fatigues—tiger suits—and some had red, white and blue bandannas around their necks. They carried a wide variety of weapons, from the Swedish K and the AR-15 to the more conventional M-16. They were unshaven, most with a three- or four-day growth. No one paid any attention to Sonny and me as we walked into the TOC. There were rows of seats placed haphazardly on a dirt floor and I sat in one, over-whelmed by the heat. There was some sort of a briefing in session: four people crouched over a chalkboard while a fifth person scratched sweeping lines with a piece of chalk. At the entrance to the TOC was a 44-gallon drum filled with beer cans floating in a slurry of ice and muddy water. And so we sat accompanied by the hiss and pop of opening beer cans as groups finished briefings only to be replaced by another.

After about half an hour during which time no one had spoken to us, I noticed a solidly built bloke lounging across two chairs next to Sonny and me. 'You the Aussies?' the man said, offering his hand. His question was obviously rhetorical as both Sonny and I wore jungle greens with Australian shoulder patches, but I refrained from making some smart-arsed remark and shook his hand. 'My name's Gritz,' he drawled, the twang of the Bible Belt South deep in his voice. He wore no badges of rank. 'Welcome, but you better get your ass over there. Your team's next.' Gritz pointed towards the group gathering in front of the board. We did as we were told, shuffling over to the chalkboard.

I sat in a daze trying to concentrate on what the team leader, Master Sergeant John Wolf, was saying. It was some sort of an ambush he was planning, but the combination of the tropical heat and a sense of detachment distracted me, so much so that I nearly missed the question until it dawned on me that Wolf was addressing me. 'You got any objections if we use you to snatch the prisoner, Cap'n?' *Snatch the prisoner? Holy shit!* I thought.

'Sure,' I responded hoping to Christ that my voice didn't betray the moiling in my guts. 'I've got no objection.'

I lay in my bunk that night in a cold sweat. Only 24 hours earlier I had been home safe in Australia and now here I was in a darkened tent on the edge of War Zone C with the whining sound of mosquitoes, contemplating the fact that at first light I would be on the ground somewhere on the border of Cambodia with a bunch of ragtag crazy Yanks and their Cambodian mercenaries. And if everything went to plan I would be required to leap out onto a jungle track we were to ambush and grab a prisoner! My heart was hammering so hard that I was startled out of my wits by a slight noise beside my bunk and, turning, caught sight of John Wolf near the tent flap. 'Thought you'd like to know we were joshing about you grabbing the prisoner, Sir.' The 'sir' rolled out like surf. 'We'll be slanting the claymores to just knock 'em off their feet.' But in the event that didn't quite happen. By nine o'clock that morning we had killed two people and captured a third who was wounded, but bled to death aboard the helicopter on his way back to the TOC.

4 THE APACHES OF BLACK VIRGIN MOUNTAIN

As my mind slips into the daily pattern of operations out of the Tay Ninh FOB, my thoughts keep coming back to the central figure that dominated this story. The man without whom there would have been no Rapid Fire: Bo Gritz. Already fast gaining a reputation, Gritz had been on his way to Dong Ba Thin just north of Cam Rahn Bay in early '65 to take over the Vietnamese Special Forces Parachute School when he was introduced to Charging Charlie Beckwith. At the time Beckwith had been in command of Delta Project, whose mission was to rescue downed aircraft crew and conduct wire-tapping missions deep in enemy-controlled areas. Gritz never did get to Dong Ba Thin, as Beckwith had him immediately reassigned to Delta.

In October '65 Gritz had been given the task of locating three NVA regiments that had mauled a Special Forces camp in the Ia Drang valley. As the NVA had taken many casualties it was assumed that they wouldn't withdraw too far before stopping to tend to their wounded. The plan was to locate the enemy and then have General Kinnard's 1st Air Cavalry Division destroy them. In the late afternoon near the Tae River,

Gritz located a field hospital containing an estimated 600 wounded together with elements of the 33rd Regiment. He and two others, Keating and Chiariello, planned to remain at an LZ they had reconnoitred nearby to guide the 1st Air Cav to the enemy's back door, but instead they were told to pull out. Apparently the 1st Air Cav would not go in without the standard aerial bombardment and preparatory gunship suppression. After the fireworks, when they finally went in, the enemy was ready for battle. The result was that the air cavalrymen had to fight one of the bloodiest and longest battles of the Vietnam War in which they lost hundreds of lives. The debacle had turned Gritz against senior officers who stuck slavishly to procedures and their minders who he called 'staff pukes', a derogatory term that is usually assigned by the Task Force to staff officers of a headquarters other than its own. The high regard his men had for him stemmed from the fact that he would never send somebody on a mission that he was not prepared to carry out himself, and his men knew it.

One afternoon chewing the rag while we were cleaning weapons among the rubber trees back at our base at Tay Ninh, John Wolf told me the story of how Gritz had interviewed his first Long Range Reconnaissance Patrol (LRRP) volunteers. 'This is no longer a volunteer unit,' Gritz had said. 'You'll be issued a lightweight body bag. A number will be stencilled on the bag to correspond with your number on the roster. I want zippers on the inside and outside. You'll use the body bag to stay dry when you sleep at night. If you're shot you'll crawl into the bag and do your best to zip it up to make recovery of your corpse easier. There are only four ways you can get out. First, you die and we ship your remains out in the bag provided. Second, you're wounded and medivacked. Third, you DEROS (return home after tour of duty), or fourth, you provide me with a suitable replacement.'

I can just see Gritz making his proclamation to a bunch of

reluctant LRRPs who had suddenly realised that this was not some posturing outfit which would give them kudos but require them to leave the safety of the base camp only rarely. There was an aura of destiny about Gritz. He trod mountain tops while the rest of us mortal men struggled in the steep valleys. It's rare to find such a man and even rarer to know two such people in one lifetime. But the freakiest thing of all is to have two of them in the one place—a bit like Napoleon rubbing shoulders with say, Attila the Hun—sometimes with near catastrophic results.

Six months before I left Canungra, Joe Mann had relinquished command of Battle Wing. His replacement, Lieutenant Colonel Ron Grey, immediately made his mark by sacking half the staff, which put the fear of God into the rest of us. He was a hard-charger who didn't mince words. I got on well with him, so much so that when he visited Vietnam on a fact-finding mission in December '67 he insisted on coming to see me. The staff officers who had prepared his itinerary were not too keen: after all, who the hell was Krasnoff? And where the hell was he anyway? But Grey was adamant and one day I was given a terse message telling me that he was on his way. As I knew what the worst-case scenario could be, I hastened to meet him as he climbed off his helicopter on arrival at Tay Ninh. After we'd greeted each other, I pulled him aside. 'Whatever you do, Sir, don't ask Gritz to *show* you what's going on here. Just hear the briefing.' Everything went well until lunch. After Grey had been given a run-down on our operations and fortified by a couple of whiskies, he turned to Gritz and said, 'Major, all that patrolling sounds pretty good, but what actually *happens* out there?'

I could feel my guts roll up into a little ball. 'Do you really mean that, Colonel? You want to know what happens?' Gritz glanced in my direction. I groaned.

'I don't say things I don't mean, Major,' Grey snapped back, sealing his fate.

Gritz just stood there for an instant, a little half-smile playing on his face before turning on his heel. 'Hey Smusch, get your team together. We've got an instant replay!' Captain Dick Smusch had joined us about ten days before. His ten-man team had hit an enemy party at first light that morning, leaving two dead NVA soldiers on the track. Smusch had booby-trapped the area and had pulled out only a few hours previously and was resting, trying to get his head together. 'Krasnoff, you better give the colonel your gear.' Gritz waved his arm in a circular motion around his head, looking in the direction of the TOC. 'Get the C&C going!' The C&C is the command and control helicopter, a UH-1H with a number of radios used to control team insertions, extractions and air support.

Gobsmacked, I found myself handing Grey my customised SLR rifle. It had a shortened barrel, carried 30-round magazines instead of the standard load and could fire automatic bursts. I couldn't believe what was happening. Grey was being fitted out with a tiger suit right there on the tarmac as the helicopter blades whirled faster and faster and the engines groaned and whined. There was confusion everywhere. The Cambodians—Bodes as we called them—were being 'policed' up by Smusch's team. Smusch was standing in utter bewilderment, his equipment hanging off his shoulders. He'd been dozing in the tropical heat and the sweat dribbled in streaks across his face as his mind tried to catch up with a world that was spinning way too fast.

'Get in the C&C.' Gritz jerked his chin in the direction of the helicopter and I followed him aboard, my mind reeling with the possibilities. I spotted Grey climbing aboard one of the slicks being loaded with members of Smusch's team. I could see myself at a court martial trying to explain why I stood by while a visiting non-combatant senior officer from Australia under *my* care was dropped on the Cambodian border and . . . what? *Wounded? Killed?* I belched the biggest gas bubble of my life as the C&C ship gathered power and took off, noticing as the slipstream flattened the shirt against my chest that the slicks carrying Smusch and his team were also lifting off. We were about to have our instant replay.

The two bodies had been lying on the track for about five hours, by which time the enemy had infiltrated about 100 men into the area so that when Smusch and his team appeared they were met with heavy ground fire. Grey was trapped on the exposed LZ. The most indelible memory I have of Grey's visit is a picture of this tubby bloke running around the trunk of a large tree with bullets impacting close by. Grey was pausing long enough to fire bursts before hot-footing it. That was the only time I was really eager to get on the ground, reckoning that I may as well go down with Grey rather than face the music back home. And Gritz obliged. He immediately ordered the C&C ship to land near the tree and as we both ran for cover it dawned on me that Grey had my rifle and I was armed with a .45 calibre automatic pistol that John Wolf told me he only ever carried to go to the john. Two hours later we were extracted. The only casualties were Dick Smusch, who was creased in the neck by a bullet, and a Bode who took a shell splinter in the leg. Ron Grey became an instant Rapid Fire legend.

Soon after that, Jim Cahill joined us. Cahill had already had a stint with Mike Force in Da Nang and the rigours of amoebic dysentery had left him gaunt and hollow-eyed but not unenthusiastic. When Gritz planned a shake-down exercise for the new LRRPs, Cahill immediately declared himself fit and joined the group. I too was given a role as a gun, which basically meant that I was to add to the firepower. The boys had been impressed with my customised SLR and had dubbed it the 'elephant gun'.

Just before last light about twenty of us were trucked to

Suoi Da, a Special Forces camp at the base of Nui Ba Den. Known as Black Virgin Mountain, Nui Ba Den was a dark, brooding, massive pyramid-shaped feature that jutted 3000 feet above sea level, dominating about 50 miles of jungle. Like a siren of Greek mythology, Nui Ba Den would lure combat troops to its bosom. Because of its dominance, its summit was occupied by a reinforced signals detachment that provided a re-broadcasting facility throughout Vietnam, and its base had Suoi Da strategically placed five miles east of Tay Ninh and 75 miles north of Saigon. And right in the middle was a hard-core VC unit.

We pulled out of Suoi Da just as the shadows blurred into darkness, following a rock-strewn track that led upwards towards Nui Ba Den. In a matter of minutes the stillness of the night was shattered by a prolonged burst of gunfire. Red tracer cracked high over our heads as our patrol rapidly changed direction and headed towards the flat ground. As we sought cover in a dry paddy field I remember thinking that red tracer means friendly fire and being momentarily comforted by that. But then it dawned on me that there was nothing protective about friendly fire. The bloody stuff could kill you just as easily! We lay in the darkness for a while with the sky stitched by red tracer before the order came to 'circle wagons'. The expression is a hangover from the days of the American Wild West and I expected to hear the blood-curdling yelps of attacking Apache Indians coming at us from the flat rim of the paddy field. I nearly choked on a fit of nervous giggling at the ludicrous thought.

About an hour later one of the LRRPs crawled up and handed me the handpiece of his radio. 'Listen to this,' he whispered. Through the static I could hear the urgent whispered conversation between the patrol commander and someone from flank security. 'Can you see it? . . . Yeah. It's a cave huh? Yeah . . . And there's folks comin' out. See them? Yeah . . . And look at that truck! Yeah . . .' Well, up until that point I was all

SHADOWS ON THE WALL

for believing that the Apache tribe was really the Vietcong and that they weren't on horseback, but were crawling out of a cave nearby. But the truck . . . well now, that really got me thinking. I slowly lifted my shoulders to get a better view, listening for the sound of a vehicle in the heavy silence. The tracer display had long ceased and the night belonged to an owl that periodically gave a mournful hoot. Beyond that I couldn't hear a damn thing. The LRRP beside me cast a quizzical glance at me. 'Can you see anything?' he whispered. I shook my head. We lay side by side for a long while, listening to the frantic whispers on the radio as the saga unfolded. The VC had produced a folding table and were holding a conference as more trucks appeared from the cave.

Finally, as the first tinge of predawn light touched the paddy field I *did* hear something. It was the stuttering sound of a motor scooter. As I squinted I could just make out the tarred shoulders of a road verging our paddy field. I realised instantly that flank security would have placed claymores to cover the road, and knew that whoever was using it would soon be within their killing range. The sound of the scooter grew as the rider approached, and I could just make out the slender shape of a Vietnamese woman wearing a floral ao dai. A conical straw hat sat squarely on her head while her long hair flowed behind her in the slipstream like oil on a rolling sea. In that instant I knew that this was not the enemy, and while the woman was in breach of the night curfew she was a non-combatant. She sat gracefully on her scooter, her ao dai painted against her thighs, her face relaxed. There was no sign of a weapon on her person or in her saddlebags. My guts churned and I winced in anticipation of the detonation of the claymores, but mercifully there was only silence as the sound of the scooter receded down the road.

Obviously the TOC had been monitoring the whispered conversations all through the night, and as the dawn light strengthened I could hear the sound of choppers. In a swirl of dust the slicks came in, disgorging tiger suits. Gritz was the first man on the spot. Later, after he'd interrogated half the patrol he swung on me. 'What the hell's goin' on out there, Krasnoff?'

I shrugged, trying to avoid his angry stare. 'I think some of the boys were seeing things,' I offered lamely. Up until that time the Task Force had a pretty lenient attitude towards the use of amphetamines, but after this incident 'brown bombers' were surely frowned upon.

5 MODUS OPERANDI AND THE CANDY BAR KID

The world's a great place if you can blot out the dreadful things human beings do to each other, especially during the madness of war. Caught up in that vortex myself, even at the time I'd wondered what the point was of our operations out of Tay Ninh. The teams were in action a lot and we were inflicting casualties on the enemy, but what intelligence were we gathering?

The Task Force had started off in Tay Ninh province in August '67 and had moved to Ham Tan and then to Phuoc Vinh for a short period before returning to Tay Ninh. Gritz had split the Task Force into two A-Teams, 361 and 362. Each of the teams had about 200 Bodes led by Special Forces troopers. Operations were based on ten-man hatchet teams tasked to ambush heavily used jungle trails in the border region of War Zone C. Each hatchet team had at least three Special Forces or LRRP troopers in it: a team leader, a communications man and a bak si, medic, but it was more usual to have four, even five to a team.

The tactic was simple but very effective: the hatchet teams would probe the border areas looking for a fight. Once the enemy responded, the Task Force would envelop them with the rest of the troops. The A-Teams rotated on patrol duty, with the off-duty team on stand-by as a reaction force for the hatchet teams on the ground in the event of trouble. And trouble came thick and fast.

And that reminds me of Dave Spencer on that day in Area of Operations (AO) Duc.

Spencer's worried. Not that he should be. He's the assistant team leader of a pretty experienced team, but the mission's one of those 'hurry up' operations, the kind that always makes you wonder if you've touched all the bases. Pridemore's the team leader and he's been given the task to search the high ground overlooking the Saigon River. The VC had recently launched 140 mm rocket attacks against the 25th Division base at Tay Ninh and the division staff was anxious to locate the enemy battery.

Spencer had been in Polk's team until a few days before when Polk was wounded and medivacked. When Pridemore had approached him, he was glad, looking forward to a change of pace—a quiet recon was just the thing after having spent a hairy few hours in the middle of an enemy base camp. 'Wesson, Miller, Song and Old Man are already on the team,' Pridemore had said. Spencer knew the two Bodes. They were older than average. Song was dubbed Big Cowboy. Both he and Old Man were dependable. Wesson was a nineteen-year-old kid going for thirty. Miller, a year younger, was still a teenager at heart and Spencer had been concerned about them drinking the night before the mission. 'Don't hit the "happy juice". We're out before dawn,' he'd said.

'We know,' Wesson had responded, unabashed.

The team's in the air—unsmiling faces, troops jammed up on the floor of the Huey. No one ever smiles going in. The chopper banks sharply and hovers over the clearing. The team spills out, runs to the edge of the jungle—tiger suits crouching, listening. Spencer keeps an eye on Old Man, the barometer of the enemy's presence.

Moving again in the dawn chill, Big Cowboy on point, Miller walking his slack, Pridemore next, followed by Old Man with the radio on his back, then Wesson and Spencer in the tail gunner position. Within seconds two VC cross the back trail moving diagonally right to left—moving fast. The team freezes. Agonising minutes pass before the enemy disappears. The team moves on.

Old Man mouths 'VC' in barely more than a whisper, pointing towards the LZ they've just vacated. The enemy is in front as well as behind the team. Big Cowboy is convinced that the VC are aware of the team's presence and are trailing them. Spencer drops back and ambushes the back trail, but sees nothing.

Just before noon when the team reaches a stream, Big Cowboy and Miller wade through the cold chest-deep water. The stream is 50 feet wide with steep mud banks and dense bamboo thickets—heavy going. Pridemore and Old Man cross next while Spencer watches the rear and Wesson keeps a sharp eye on the flanks. As Spencer enters the water he can hear Wesson floundering behind him, stuck in some fallen bamboo. With Spencer's help Wesson extricates himself and both of them cross the stream. The team holes up, wedged against the bank while Pridemore sends a situation report. Some of them take the opportunity to eat their midday meal.

'Watcha got there, Davey?' Wesson whispers and Spencer grins back at him as he unwraps the candy bar, leaning back against the base of a huge tree.

'Vanilla cream bar.'

'Screw you,' Wesson mumbles, losing interest as he realises that Spencer is not about to share the candy.

Spencer points the muzzle of his M-16 in the direction of Wesson's area of responsibility, reminding him of the need to keep watch. 'You snooze, you lose,' he whispers. Old Man is crouched close to Spencer and suddenly his eyes widen a little. He thrusts past Spencer, letting go a long burst across the stream, cursing in Cambodian the entire time.

Bullets thump into Spencer's tree as he struggles to bring his M-16 into play, but the selector switch is jammed! Rolling on his side, he snatches a spare magazine and uses it to bang the selector switch to the 'fire' position while Big Cowboy and Pridemore fire bursts into the bamboo. Pridemore's flat on the ground, talking on the radio while Big Cowboy and Miller chop up the bamboo. Wesson's firing short bursts across the creek.

'We're going to Maguire rig out!' Pridemore shouts, smacking Spencer on the leg to get his attention. 'You go first!'

Spencer shakes his head. 'Wesson and Miller should go first.'

'No,' Pridemore shouts back. 'You and Wesson go first.'

Old Man is still probing the back trail with searching fire.

'Pop smoke!' Pridemore yells and Spencer pulls the pin and pitches a smoke grenade along the back trail. A yellow cloud billows around the dense bamboo. There's the sound of a hovering chopper and the looped rope of a Maguire rig drops through the canopy with the impact of a fat lady crashing through a skylight.

'Wesson!' Spencer yells over the sound of battle. Wesson crawls over and squats in one of the looped cargo straps that serve as a makeshift seat while Spencer tries furiously to untangle the snarled ropes. Pridemore, Miller and the two Bodes are trying to hold back the VC as Spencer works at freeing the ropes. 'Fuck this!' Spencer stands upright in frustration, ignoring the sound of incoming rounds.

Handwerk's the belly man lying flat on the floor of the chopper. He's screaming at Spencer to get out of the way so that he can cut the tangled ropes, but no one hears him. The rope slams down into the trees, tangling Spencer like a kitten with a ball of yarn.

The chopper is taking hits now.

'We've gotta get to an LZ.' Pridemore points roughly towards the south-east. 'You're on point,' he yells, glancing at Spencer with his 'and don't let me down' look.

The line of march is right across the bend in the stream. Spencer yells for Wesson to follow him and slides down the steep bank into the muddy water. As he starts across the stream, he feels the wallop of an underwater explosion. There's water raining down on him and his eardrums feel as if they've burst. *Grenade. The bastards have dropped a grenade in the water,* he thinks as he flounders across the stream, vaguely noticing the waterspouts that erupt around him. A crumpled form detaches itself from the cover of the far bank and slides limply into the water. The body floats by, strangely at peace. Spencer spots a muzzle flash from the far bank like a candle flickering in the jungle and instinctively fires at it. He senses rather that sees the far bank and crawls up on the shore. They're still firing at him, the whipcracking sound of the bullets audible even to his injured eardrums. Dazed, he gives covering fire as the others cross the stream. He crashes through the bamboo and breaks out into open ground—it's the LZ! He covers the ground as the rest of the patrol break out of the jungle. Pridemore sets up perimeter defence in the centre of the clearing and the patrol awaits the slicks as gunships rake the surrounding jungle.

Back at the FOB Spencer limps off to have his leg attended. There's a deep gash in it. As the Bode medic probes his wound, he mutters something about splinters. Spencer doesn't register.

A year later Spencer develops a boil-like lump on his shin. One morning he wakes up to discover that during the night his lump has given birth to a piece of iron the size of a nail clipping—a legacy of AO Duc.

There's no way the teams on the ground can survive without the air assets placed in direct support of our operations.

As well as a C&C ship with radios Gritz also had, under command, a light-fire team: two UH-1H Huey helicopters mounted with 20 mm cannon and air-to-ground rockets. Four Iroquois helicopters provided a rapid deployment capability, but that's all that was provided. Because B-36 was only listed as a provisional unit, Uncle Sam was a bit mean-fisted about the rest and we had to scrounge for food and liquor using captured weapons for barter. What couldn't be obtained through barter was simply stolen and we had some past masters at this game. Aleo, who was the unofficial purser, was legendary. He could steal a radio while it was playing and leave the music in the room. All the vehicles used in the camp had been 'appropriated', their numbers repainted to represent various ARVN units. A strongly partisan attitude prevailed in B-36. If you weren't a member of the Task Force you were the enemy and your equipment was fair game.

But back to our modus operandi: Gritz would earmark an area of operations and the Task Force would deploy daily, remaining in that area for three to four weeks depending on enemy activity. The codename for Task Force operations was Rapid Fire and a grouping of areas was designated by Roman numerals. I had joined the unit during Rapid Fire IV and remained with them until Rapid Fire VI. In the period before Rapid Fire V the Task Force had achieved significant results. We had captured documents that indicated that the VC was getting NVA replacements to bolster their numbers. For instance the 52nd VC Artillery Regiment had been receiving re-inforcements from the north for many months and it was now taking the NVA only 90 days to do the trip from North Vietnam to War Zone C instead of 120. We learnt the hard way that our own regular troops' reaction into War Zone C was at best tentative and often non-existent. In September '67 the Task Force located the 274th VC Regiment but the US 9th Division took too long to react and the enemy melted into the jungle. Documents and weapons captured by the Rapid Fire patrol indicated that the 274th had recently been in Cambodia. The dead VC had Cambodian money and carried Cambodian 'fish' (marijuana). Their weapons, principally AK-47s, were new and there were indications that the regiment had recently been re-supplied and reinforced from the north. Further contacts in October determined the presence of the 271st VC Regiment in Minh Tanh. A Rapid Fire patrol killed the commander of the 1st Battalion of the 271st and his executive officer. But it was Rapid Fire V that sticks clearly in my mind. This was the operation that led us to the NVA forces massing on the Cambodian border.

Much later, while studying the Indochina war from the perspective of the enemy, I came upon a series of events that inevitably put the Task Force on a collision course with Hanoi's forces. William J. Duiker's book, *Ho Chi Minh,* provided pieces of the jigsaw. On 20 December 1960, deep in the jungles of Tay Ninh province near an area of rubber plantations, the National Liberation Front (NLF) had been established. Ton Duc Thang, a party elder, described it as an alliance of all classes, including all religious and ethnic minorities of South Vietnam, with its purpose to create a unified Vietnam. The NLF was organised into various echelons from a central committee down to cells at the village level. To handle military operations the Central Office for South Vietnam (COSVN), the old southern branch of the Central Committee that had operated during the Franco-Vietminh war, was secretly re-established. The military arm of this organisation was called the People's Liberation Armed Forces or, as the Saigon regime called it, the Viet Cong. In October '61 the Central Committee decided that tit-for-tat operations against the militarily strong United States of America would not succeed as they had against the French, and that guerilla warfare should be utilised. By 1963 the Central Committee, guided by General Nguyen Chi Thanh and Le Duan, confirmed the concept of increased guerilla warfare and over 5000 troops from North Vietnam were infiltrated into the south that year. Moved by truck into the mountains of southern Laos and then on foot over jungle trails that had been hacked out during the war against the French, the northerners were met by local Viet Cong and guided to destinations within South Vietnam. The complex of trails was known to the world as the Ho Chi Minh Trail. By the spring of '66 North Vietnamese regular forces were being infiltrated into the south in significant numbers to match the US build-up and a plan was hatched for a popular general uprising to be initiated, beginning 31 January 1968. This was to be the Tet (Vietnamese Lunar New Year) Offensive. Little did we know at the time that the enemy had infiltrated 4000 troops into Cholon, the Chinese sector of Saigon.

The trek from North Vietnam was a tortuous one, fraught with much adversity, as described in *Ho Chi Minh* by some of those who participated: 'The farther south we got, the worse our situation became. Finally we were down to a few kilos of rice. For two months we ate what we could find in the jungle— leaves, roots, animals and birds. At first we would walk eight hours a day, but with the climbing and the jungle, it was slow going. When and where we rested depended on our guide and our leader, but even the way-stations were not like some stopover in the city. There was nothing to shelter you from the rain. You just put up your hammock and slept in it. The way-stations were supposed to have food and water, but they were often short. So each individual learned to save his own rations. The further we went, the worse the hunger we faced. As food grew shorter comradeship broke down. We became intent on saving our own lives.'

6

EAGLE FLIGHTS AND PICNIC OUTINGS

EAGLE FLIGHTS AND
PICNIC OUTINGS

Thinking about the enemy brings to mind the African dung beetle. It's that little insect that spends most of its life in darkness digging up buffalo shit and the like on the veldt. The regular Viet Cong and NVA units were like a whole lot of dung beetles trying to survive in a hostile environment where massive airpower was thrown against them. The NVA were a long way from home, strangers who could not easily escape detection. To compensate for this they stayed away from villages and dug holes, living in darkness, building bunker complexes that stretched the length of the country. Every rotten piece of jungle had its complex: bays with overhead protection linked by trenches and spider holes. Movement for the NVA was from one bunker system to the next, all the way down the flank of the orange peel that was South Vietnam. You could be standing on top of the bunkers and not know; that's how well they were camouflaged. In any event, not all the bunkers were occupied so it was very much a hit-and-miss operation trying to winkle them out.

In this winkling process, the Task Force would sometimes

employ a tactic of using 'eagle flights' where the C&C ship would fly low in an attempt to draw ground fire while the slicks, loaded with troops, hovered out of sight at high altitude. Once a target had been located, the eagle flight would fall out of the sky on top of it, a different tactic from the usual one where teams were first put on the ground to find the enemy. It was during one of those missions, about three weeks after I'd arrived, that John Wolf was wounded. We'd received fire in the initial insertion, landing virtually on top of a bunker system, but we were lucky. It was only a caretaker unit in occupation. Documents captured showed it to be part of the VC C 19 Engineer Battalion that had been tasked to carry out repair work as a result of bomb damage. On 30 November, in a firefight that lasted for almost an hour, Wolf took a bullet in the stomach and a dustoff—medivack helicopter—flew him, along with a number of wounded Bodes, to the hospital at Cu Chi. We had four Bodes killed that day, which weighed heavily on all of us. Wolf's shoes were hard to fill in the hatchet team.

Master Sergeant John Wolf clucked and fussed over his brood so much he was nicknamed 'Mother' by his contemporaries. A devout Catholic, he used to kneel by his cot in prayer every night before going to bed and I rarely heard him use a swear word in all the time I knew him. Yet this mild-mannered man was a thorough professional, which I suppose emphasises the point that appearances are often deceiving.

But we weren't always out in the jungle. Some of the time was spent in the base camp. The rubber plantation at Tay Ninh stretched into the distance, rows of neglected trees that hadn't been tapped in a long time. The trees, however, were being used for another purpose. It was convenient for hatchet teams to test-fire their weapons into them and many were showing signs of stress, their olive-green leaves curling and turning brown.

Gritz had been unconcerned about the damage until somebody pointed out that the plantation belonged to Air

Marshall Nguyen Cao Ky, the President of South Vietnam, and there was a possibility that the US government could be handed a hefty bill for compensation. 'I know how to fix the problem,' says Gritz. 'We'll have a firefight.' The plan was simple: a group would slip out in front of our position with captured AK-47s and SKSs and open fire. In the ensuing exchange of fire some rubber trees would obviously be hit. The incident would be recorded as an enemy probe—end of problem.

In between hatchet missions, I had been given the task of supervising the digging of slit trenches in the rubber adjacent to the tents. The base had been operational for about twelve weeks and with the constant activity there was a strong possibility of being mortared by the enemy. Perhaps I was given that job because of my great expertise, having been a member of Battle Wing at the Jungle Training Centre. More likely, it was probably because the boys thought I'd make a good slave driver. That's bullshit too. I probably got the job because no one else wanted it and there was no way I could pull rank. Gritz was the Major and he sat at the right hand of God. The rest of us were just part of the team and we squatted where we could, and being relatively new my place in the pecking order was one seat north of the outhouse. Anyway, it gave me an opportunity to get to know some of the Bodes.

I have the utmost admiration for the Bodes. Unlike most of us who would rotate back home after a stint in Vietnam, these people were lifers. I remember asking Pak, who was an interpreter and later became my 'bodyguard', what he thought about the less than rosy prospects of the Bodes in the Task Force. 'Sin loi dai hui—tough luck, Captain,' Pak had said, shrugging his shoulders with that typically Asian expression of stoicism which just about encapsulated the Bodes' attitude. They were born to hard times, under the hammer with both the South Vietnamese and the Viet Cong. I also grew to respect their skill at arms. Suol and Huon were marksmen with the

M-16, every bit as good as any riflemen I knew. Danh, who had been wounded during Blackjack-33 and had returned to serve in the Task Force, was as good a silent weapons specialist as I've seen. At first I had been critical of the Bode leadership. It seemed to me that clear-cut orders were never given and what sounded like a village squabble would occur every time instructions were passed on. I despaired, assuming that vital information would be lost somewhere in the heated wrangling that went on. However, on the occasions when I observed people like platoon leader Thinh in action I was much impressed. The soldiers knew what they had to do and did it without objection. As things became more familiar between us, the Bodes began to use my nickname. I was called Crazy Horse but the Bodes couldn't get their tongue around the 'horse' bit so I finished up with Crazy Hor. There you have it, the Task Force ended up calling me Crazy Whore.

The trench-digging task had been finished just before the scheduled enemy probe and as I rested beside one of the trenches awaiting the fireworks I was joined by Bernie Newman and Patrick 'Hulk' Martin—both members of 361. Bernie Newman was a lean and mean master sergeant with a gap-toothed smile and a yuk-yuk chuckle. The thing about soldiers on operations is that they're very perceptive. You get to cut to the chase when you don't know how much time you have on this plot and the odds are against you. Bernie had a resonant voice and was aptly nicknamed Sergeant Snorkle. He had chalked up two tours of duty at the time I met him and lived from one adrenalin high to the next. As we rested beside the trench he nudged the Hulk. 'Tell Krasnoff about Operation Picnic,' he said.

I'd heard about Picnic and knew that Newman was referring to an operation on the Bien Soi River that had occurred before my arrival. I glanced at the Hulk. If you picture a Viking without the horned cap and fur coat you've got the Hulk:

cropped blond hair and a barrel chest on a bloke that stood at least six two. Well, apart from the Viking, the outfit resembled a swashbuckling minorities' convention with African, Mexican and Cuban-Americans. And there were a couple of French-Americans thrown in as well. Ritchie, or FM as he was called, had been wounded and was in Cu Chi hospital, thereby diminishing the international flavour by one Japanese-American. There was even an American Indian, Jerry Fairweather, who was a natural at this job. As well as a couple of Mafia *soldati*. OK, just kidding although Aleo *was* nicknamed the Wop.

My attention returned to Bernie and the Hulk. 'It was my first firefight,' said Hulk. 'The forward scout, Phuong Kiet, hadn't gone more than five steps when the shit hit the fan. I felt him yanking on my trouser cuffs and when he finally got my attention I realised that the white scars appearing on the tree trunks were bullet creases. First fucking lesson—incoming fire always has right of way! I was just paralysed, shit cracking all around me. With all the stuff going on it dawned on me that Major Gritz should know. I told him we had a wonderful firefight on our hands and kind of invited him to join us. I guess I sort of went berserk. I don't remember a whole lot. I remember charging, screaming, the wrong way into the second squad and throwing Bodes up on line. I guess I scared them more than the enemy because they all charged the camp. Kim fired his M-79 grenade launcher at such a close range there was no explosion, but the projectile split an NVA soldier's skull. That was lucky. That dude had been holding the firing device to a large Chinese platter mine.'

'Yeah, and I chewed his ass out for the way he sent that goddamned situation report,' Newman grumbled, looking pointedly at the Hulk. 'We were damn lucky.' He shook his head. 'We could hear the firefight and guessed it was the Hulk and his recon platoon so we just ran towards the firing. There was this bamboo gate in the jungle and all these voices, sounded like the fucking Super Bowl . . .' Bernie paused. 'I think there was some kind of a show going on, you know? . . . like entertainment. Anyhow Critchley's yelling at me, something about Clyde (the VC) being on the other side of a mound and then there's this deafening roar of machine-gun fire and I'm flat on my face in the mud.'

Critchley was the nickname the Task Force had given Ken Crichton, a Canadian airborne company commander Gritz had recruited into the MGF. Critchley had resigned from the Canadian Army to serve as an NCO and had eventually been promoted in the field to captain in B-36. I'd met this little old grey-haired bloke at Tay Ninh when I first arrived and remembered thinking: what's this old fart doing here? In fact Critchley was in his late thirties. He told me one day that he'd gone grey overnight. He'd been wounded with the MGF during Operation Blackjack in May '67. 'He'll get you killed,' Critchley had muttered in his clipped accent, a blend of North American and Pommy English, darting a quick glance at Bo Gritz.

'When we broke through I could see that recon had taken heavy casualties. There were tiger suits all over the place,' Newman paused. 'The secondary growth had been removed in a space that could house around 600 people. There were three times the number of Viet Cong dead, all around the humps of underground bunkers and the zigzag trench that ran around the perimeter.' Newman's eyes lit up. 'We caught the fuckers with their pants down.' He chuckled. 'Tell Krasnoff about the well,' he said as an afterthought.

I'd heard Gritz tell that story, but this was coming from the horse's mouth. 'I don't know what happened to my rifle but it wasn't in my hands as three VC leapt out of a bunker right into my arms. There wasn't much I could do except grab them all and dump them down an open well only a step away. They thrashed around and yelled so much I pitched a grenade in and took off after Bernie, the Major and the Amazing Spiderman.' Hulk paused, gathering his thoughts. 'Too many of the Bodes were stopped by hostile fire at the first trench line. The cost was high but we had won. Among the lessons learnt that day was the value of attacking by way of the enemy's outhouse.' Hulk smiled. 'You know, we really kicked ass. I never felt so good since I met my wife.' All three of us laughed, but I sensed the understatement in the Hulk's story.

No pun intended, but Operation Picnic had obviously been no picnic. For a long time the A-Team detachment at Bien Soi had been concerned about a large enemy formation on the north side of the Bien Soi River. No one had ventured into the enemy stronghold despite the frequent air strikes. The detachment commander had mentioned his concern during Gritz's visit to the camp, describing the mounting enemy pressure his fortified camp was experiencing. At the time Gritz was looking for a suitable location for a shake-down operation for his new unit and this seemed an ideal opportunity. He had previously been pressured by the 25th Infantry Division to get into the area and now took the opportunity to inform the divisional intelligence officer, Major Mayo, that while B-36 didn't have the time to 'ricochet around' for too long, he *would* dedicate a weekend to find and fix the enemy headquarters. One Saturday in August '67 Gritz assembled the Task Force and announced that they would all be trucked to a secret location on the river, board an LCVP landing craft and spend the evening floating silently downstream. At dawn they would disembark for 'dinner on the ground and an all-day sing'.

'The thing that grabbed my attention,' Newman growled, 'was here we were in the middle of this fucking bunker system and Major Gritz turns to Crichton and says, "Critch, you consolidate the camp. Get your guys into the trenches. We can expect an all out counterattack in the next few minutes. My guess is we're occupying a regimental headquarters and it won't take Charlie long to muster the battalions. I'll get Ritchie headed this way." Critch takes off after the Hulk and here I am with the lone radio operator and bodies strewn from the gate all the way to the bunkers. Suddenly bedlam breaks out to our east. For a moment I thought the enemy had begun to counterattack but the range was too great. Then it hit me— Ritchie had run into the enemy incoming to our defence.'

Many years later, in email conversation with Jim Donahue, a platoon leader in 362 during Picnic I, I gained a better perspective on what happened to Ritchie's force as it went to the rescue of 361. Donahue had left Vietnam about eight weeks prior to my arrival and had been on the Blackjack operation (described in his book *Blackjack-33*). He had this to say: 'We were moving inland from the river when 361 was hit. Jim Condon, Larry Rader, Ray Fratus and David Spencer with about ten LRRPs were set up in a blocking force when 361 radioed Captain Ritchie for help. We took off then, moving in two columns. I was point man in the left column and Bill Ferguson was running point on the right. "Head for the firing," Ritchie yelled, and that's what we were doing—hauling ass. We were hit by heavy automatic fire and that's when I heard the radio . . . Fergy had been hit, and I started crawling in his direction . . . I'm not sure what the hell happened then, other than it felt like I was butt stroked. I remember firing a burst and killing a VC. I was rushing around putting the Bodes on line when our chief Cambode medic told me I was bleeding and he stuck a dressing to the back of my head. When I reached Fergy, I could see that he had multiple wounds. The bullet that killed him had hit him in the eye, moved through the roof of his mouth and ended up somewhere in his trunk. I had Fergy in a fireman's carry but he was so darn tall—feet and hands dragging on the ground . . . We were pulling out and Fergy and I were being left behind . . .

'Fergy and I finished up in an overgrown bomb crater when

I saw a number of VC moving past on both sides of us. They hadn't seen us. Then there was a heap of firing and I watched some of the VC running back towards us. I shot them as they drew level with us. I finally made it to the river where Bo and the rest of them had formed a base. They were calling in heavy artillery from Tay Ninh . . . Yeah . . . Finally we were picked up by boat and taken to Ben Soi and then Trang Sup.'

The story goes that when Gritz broke into Ritchie's defensive perimeter after it had been counterattacked by the VC, Ritchie's first words were, 'I want to court-martial this whole damn bunch!' To which Gritz had asked, 'Why in God's name do you want to do that?'

Ritchie had replied, 'Every one of 'em's wounded. I call a medivack to take 'em out. None of 'em want to go. I had to order them on to the dustoff. They put the wounded Bodes on instead. I call for a second medivack, nobody would get abroad.'

After the first medivack chopper took off with the Bodes the wounded Americans refused to get on the chopper. Captain Ritchie issued a direct order for everyone to get aboard. Everyone crawled into the cabin and when Ritchie looked away they crawled out the far door. When the chopper took off, Ritchie appeared shocked to see everyone standing there. 'I gave you an order to get on that chopper,' he yelled.

'You did,' Duke replied, 'but you didn't say we had to stay on it.'

When asked by Gritz what this was all about, Duke Snider had said, 'Sir, it was like this, with all these new LRRPs we didn't figure we should leave the Captain all by himself. There ain't none of us hurt that bad.' In fact some of the wounds were horrific. Ferguson had been killed, James Battle, Ritchie's commo sergeant nearly had his arm taken off by a heavy machine gun bullet and all the rest—Snider, Cole, Hagey, Rader and Donahue—had bullet and shell fragment wounds.

In the wash-up, the Task Force had taken heavy casualities. I was mindful of the fact that, while the VC would vigorously follow up our patrols, they rarely attempted to hold ground. In the case of Rapid Fire I, the Task Force had hit a VC district headquarters and the enemy response *should* have been a salutary lesson for me in the coming days.

I was deep in thought pondering just how close the unit had been to total annihilation when the sound of an AK-47 firing a sustained burst through the rubber trees at our Tay Ninh FOB prompted me to move to the newly dug trenches.

Just on dark, and under the supervision of Frank Hillman, the Task Force sergeant major, and Beatty, the unit's quartermaster and intelligence sergeant, a shooting party opened up in the general direction of B-32, a Special Forces detachment based on the edge of Tay Ninh. We were treated to a fireworks display of arching green tracer while our own Bodes in the front trenches responded with snarling bursts of M-16 fire. So good was the show that the local ruff puff security post at the end of the runway reported seeing a platoon of VC skulking off into the darkness. We laughed till our sides ached. But that was after the event. As I sat in the crumbly moist soil sucking on my Schlitz—I would've given anything for a Fourex—I though how lucky we had been with the relatively few casualties since my arrival.

All that changed a few days later.

7 URI AND THE MANNLICHER SCHOENAUER

I take a deep breath. My mental foray into the jungles of Tay Ninh has left me agitated and I seek a momentary respite. It's calmer here in the warm sunshine of Hastings Street where motes of dust sparkle in the brilliant light. There's a muted clicking of china as the waitress clears away the table next to me—a comforting, rational sound. However, I'm barely able to register the tranquil setting, my mind drawing inexorably back towards . . . towards those final days at Tay Ninh.

Rapid Fire V . . . For weeks now, the start-up groan of the Hueys had heralded the dawn—a rosy light that scarcely penetrated the mist blanketing the rubber trees. Beyond the strip and the rows of trees out there in the jungle was Nui Ba Den, and somewhere west of there our infiltration points. My team had gone back to the same spot where . . . where the Face was hit. Two high mounds beside the track marked VC burial sites in the jungle mist—a shiver had run up and down my back. On the operations map in the TOC the infiltration points were marked as innocuous blue circles. But on the ground . . .

On the ground it was madness. Whenever we struck we did

so with maximum speed, designed to overwhelm and shock the enemy. Everything was up front. Essentially it was a bluff, and bluffing is a high-risk activity. What we were doing was not that different from a game of poker. As a poker player I rarely resorted to bluffing. I'm not predisposed to that sort of all-or-nothing mentality and prefer to play the odds. However, on the odd occasion that I did so I picked my moments carefully. There are some guidelines that a poker player ignores only at his peril. For instance it's advisable to try a bluff at a time when the other players believe you are having a run of luck. But in the case of Rapid Fire—to redirect the analogy—we were the lone player in War Zone C and it was only a matter of time before the enemy woke up to our game. Gritz, however, was a past master at upping the ante. As a child on Tubabao I had witnessed a similar act—a breathtaking bluff—and been struck by its audacity, against the odds.

Once every five weeks or so we had an unwelcome visitor to our island in the form of a sea-going canoe laden with Hukbalahap. The Hukbalahap, or Huk as they were called, were local communist guerillas and about eight of them would arrive on the beach. While they traded with the fishermen from the village next to our camp they would set up some speakers and harangue the locals with their propaganda. None of us refugees could understand Tagalog, the Filipino language, but it was easy to discern the thrust of their words. The Huk were hostile, warning the fishermen not to trade with the imperialist foreigners who had encroached upon their shores. This didn't really bother us. Occasionally we bought bananas from the fishermen and a few of the adults sometimes bought tuba—an alcoholic brew made from coconut milk. What bothered us was the fact that with every fresh visit, the Huk had become increasingly emboldened. Some of them took to snooping around our tent lines, and they were armed and potentially dangerous. The risk of theft or even rape compelled the group of elders, of which Pop was one, to visit the Chief of Police in Cebu city. While the chief was sympathetic, he claimed not to have the manpower to help us. After some discussion he finally acquiesced to the private sale of one World War II vintage four point deuce mortar with four rounds of ammunition, and one antiquated Mannlicher Schoenauer 27 calibre carbine. The weapons had cost us dearly. Most of the refugees had escaped Shanghai with little more than the clothes they stood in. A few had some family heirlooms—gold watches and jewellery—and these had to be sacrificed to pay the chief.

Seeing Pop had been an artillery officer during the revolution, it was natural that he was given charge of the mortar. And he took his responsibility seriously, plotting targets on the beach the Huk used when they visited the island. Because of a shortage of ammunition, Pop had been unable to verify his target plots and this dilemma preoccupied his waking hours. He spent time explaining to me how to work out his range table using nothing more than a matchbox. At the time I was uninterested, thinking the whole exercise boring, but I guess Pop was searching for support, having been given the responsibility of the camp's security at such great cost. In any event, he needn't have worried.

On the next day the Huk arrived and set up their loudspeakers, Pop waited until the beach was clear and then fired one mortar round. I can still remember the silence that followed the mortar's loud detonation with all those upturned faces, eyes riveted on the bomb that soared into the clear blue sky before reaching the height of its trajectory and plummeting to earth. The bomb exploded in a geyser of muddy water at the edge of the coral reef not far from the hull of the motorised canoe, and Pop quickly adjusted the four point deuce, slipping another round down the spout.

Bang! But this time there was pandemonium on the beach. There were Huk running in all directions, yelling as they went.

In the midst of this confusion and on the heels of the second explosion that sent bits of coral and mud spattering against the hull of the canoe, Uri appeared. In his arms he gripped the newly procured carbine, and as he charged towards the beach his eyes were agleam. 'Ooraah!' he yelled at the top of his lungs, tripping and stumbling down the uneven slope past the coconut grove. The Huk wasted no time in getting off the beach. They were gone long before the 'cavalry' arrived, spurred on no doubt by the thought of the madman who was prepared to charge in the face of mortar fire. The thing is, I don't believe there was any ammunition for the carbine, so I wondered what Uri would have done had he reached the canoe before the Huk had departed.

Whenever I recollect the incident with the mortar and Uri's charge, I wonder what effect those two would have had on Bo Gritz. If you could set a time warp and transport Pop and Uri to Tay Ninh province, I reckon Gritz would have welcomed them with open arms.

I guess in some ways Pop and I were strangers. It's not that we didn't get on. Pop was preoccupied with his own agenda, and the year my mother left him he was even less communicative. He was a good provider in the material sense. Whatever he had, he would share, but his ambition had always been to return to Russia and when that possibility faded he became increasingly despondent. I didn't often have in-depth conversations with him; however, I remember one particular occasion soon after my mother had left.

We'd been living in Australia for about four years and it was after one of Pop's frequent arguments with Uglichinin. Pop worked for Uglichinin in his furniture factory as a paymaster, which was a boon because good jobs were hard to come by. Uglichinin was a master craftsman who was quickly gaining a reputation. I visited his factory one day and those beautiful pieces made of black bean and mahogany with barley sugar twist and ball-and-claw legs looked as if they belonged in some stately home. Anyhow, Uglichinin's first name was George—actually it was Gheorgi—but no Aussie ever called him that. They didn't call him by his surname either; it was far too difficult to pronounce. So, Uglichinin became George, his furniture business became George Bros and he was formally known as Mister George.

Mister George came from the Caucasus Mountains. He was a dark complexioned Georgian with a beaked nose and the fierce eyes of a Turk. When stirred he had a fiery temper, and Pop often managed to stir him. Mister George had left Russia after the Revolution, making his way to Australia via Europe, and that was the nub of the problem between them. Pop had escaped into China in 1921 after the collapse of the White Army. He had spent 28 years in China living for the day of the counter-revolution that would sweep the communists out of Mother Russia. He saw himself at the forefront of such a movement and any Russian who shirked his responsibilities to the counter-revolution was, in Pop's eyes, a traitor to the cause. Mister George definitely fitted into that mould, for he had readily adopted Australia, abandoning the notion of ever seeing Russia again.

'Kapitalisti!' Pop had fumed, pouring himself a generous shot of brandy. His lips were a thin bloodless line of annoyance. 'All they can think of is making money. They have no dousha—(soul) . . . That bloody bastard (it came out blaati basta) . . .' Pop's English was good but heavily accented. He glared at the door. I could hear Mister George's footsteps as he climbed up the steep staircase. You didn't have to be a brain surgeon to realise against whom Pop was venting his spleen. We rented the downstairs section of Mister George's home in Camp Hill and living under our benefactor's roof always made me uncomfortable about these fights.

Pop downed the brandy and fixed himself another. 'Money.

That's all there is to that fool's life!' Pop had thundered. I was fourteen and very interested in girls and, hell, I couldn't see anything wrong with having a few bucks, particularly as I thought it might make me more attractive in the eyes of the fairer sex. Or hoped it would, more to the point.

8 JUST ANOTHER DAY AT THE OFFICE

December 30, 1967.

The little shops and teahouses in Tay Ninh are deserted in the midday heat. Even the old fan-tan players who regularly gather by the pockmarked and crumbling stucco fence on the edge of the tarmac have disappeared. It's 'pot time' and the streets are empty.

The patrol had been scheduled for debriefing in the TOC, but because of the heat it had found itself in the shade of the rubber trees just outside. There are five of them sprawled on the ground, steam rising from sweat-sodden backs, their weapons and equipment beside them: Jim Cahill, Bac Si Burr, Bernie Newman, Forester Grant and Sergeant Major Hillman. The intelligence officer (IO) doing the debriefing squats at a discreet distance because the rancid smell of sweat and dissipating tension coming from the patrol is overpowering. There's another reason why the IO holds back. The young lieutenant's pressed green fatigues, black cloth badges of rank and insignia, and spit-shined boots mark him as a 'shoeclerk' and he feels uncomfortable in the presence of the patrol. A shoe-clerk is one step better than a staff puke. The IO has just come up from Long Hai and would give anything to stay with the Task Force at Tay Ninh, but for the moment he has to be content with base camp duties.

The patrol had been twelve: six Bodes had already returned to their hooches, the seventh stands guard over a blindfolded and bound prisoner who sits dangling his feet over the edge of a nearby trench. Head bowed, the prisoner has a pull-strip of dried blood tracking from hairline to chin. His right leg is bandaged, the stark white cloth contrasting with the black pyjama trouser-leg which had been slit to allow Burr to work on the bullet wound. Burr is both medic and patrol leader. He is the only African-American medic in the Task Force and is also a permanent team leader in 361.

The patrol members look shagged, rapidly dropping off their adrenalin high. Newman has taken over command of 361, replacing Captain Dan Swain when he finished his tour of duty. Swain had been much admired by the men, but Newman was quickly imposing his own brand of leadership. Because of shortages in experienced men, Newman had slotted himself on the patrol to take up the slack.

Bernie Newman's association with the jungle is reminiscent of the bloke in the Listerine ad who hates the taste but loves the result when he washes his mouth out every morning. Just before he attended the Jungle Operations School in Panama, Newman had read Chapman's *The Jungle is Neutral*, and the book left a deep impression on him. He once told me that in his opinion more American officers should read Chapman's book rather than *The Street Without Joy* by Bernard Fall, which was mandatory reading at the time. Fall's book had, in part, led to an aversion towards ambushing by many regular units.

Burr nods to Newman indicating that he wants him to start, and so Newman is doing most of the talking, his face a running mask of camouflage cream with a roadmap of sweat. 'The VC started off from my side on the left flank, I could hear them, but something must have spooked them.'

'Yeah, Bernie can hear an ant pissing cotton at 100 yards,' Hillman growls.

'Anyhow, they moved around to our rear and then came down the track from the opposite side, five of 'em . . .' Newman pauses, his eyes cutting to Cahill. 'Jimmy here was right flank security.'

'I saw them first,' Cahill rasps, leaning back against his pack. 'I was going to let the first couple through and then Obe moved . . . '

'Where was Obe?' the IO interrupts.

'He was with me.' Cahill pulls a face as he tries to make himself comfortable against the jutting angles of his pack. He pokes distractedly at his mud-spattered boots with a twig. 'Obe moved. Charlie saw him and I shot Charlie.'

'Jimmy here wounded the first one.' Newman takes up the story.

I knew what had happened. The same was happening in 362 as well. The Bode attrition rate was so high that there was hardly enough time to train the reinforcements. In fact most of the training was OJT—on the job. One of the most important things in an ambush was to discipline oneself to keep perfectly still. Unlike the Bu Dop enlistees, our more recent recruits had come from Saigon. Some of these 'Saigon Commandos' had little patience and few field training skills, having cut their teeth on the streets of Cholon fighting the Vietnamese mafia, many of whom ran the bars and brothels on Tudo Street. Rule of thumb was: if the Bode survived four missions he'd go on to be a good soldier.

'I hit the claymores.' Cahill shrugs. He has 120 days to go in-country, and normally this would count for something in the morale stakes, but not in this job. In this job 24 hours is a lifetime. 'That's how we got the rest,' Cahill adds.

'All except that one,' Newman adds, gesturing in the direction of the prisoner. He fishes in the pouches of his webbing, tossing a frayed wallet and some dog-eared sheets of folded paper towards the IO. '141st VC Regiment.'

'All of them were armed?' the IO asks.

'Oh yeah. They were armed alright.' Burr pats the AK-47 slung over his shoulder. 'We got three more of those.' He jerks his head in the direction that Hillman and Grant are sitting.

Hillman had been in the kill zone with Burr, Grant in rear security guarding the back door. I can imagine what whould have gone through Grant's mind as the enemy probed the rear. How close had he been to firing wildly as the surreptitious noises ravaged his raw nerves?

I knew the routine. Soon as they cleaned up, the five of them would be at the B-32 bar. Just a couple of drinks in the hope that Mister Beam or Mister Daniel would induce sleep, obliterate the mind at least for a few hours. There'd be no carousing, just five people with glassy-eyed expressions quietly at the bar. At first light they'd be back on deck as part of the ready reaction force waiting for God knows what another day would bring.

9 SUTRAS AND A PRELUDE OF THINGS TO COME

January 5, 1968.

The expression 'dry season' is a misnomer. Certainly in the dry season one is spared the incessant lashing monsoon rain that turns creeks into raging torrents and the jungle into a sea of mud, but when it rains in the 'dry' it still rains heavily, if not for long.

The four coffins took pride of place at the front of the parade. Each was draped with a bright yellow cloth and as the rain fell in heavy ponderous drops, the cloth changed colour. Large dappled spots appeared that eventually fused into a nondescript khaki. The rain that fell on the parade also put out the candles surrounding each coffin. As we stood in a soggy file, tiger suits and bush hats dripping, I couldn't help thinking that the Task Force looked a sombre lot beneath the leaden sky on the edge of the airstrip; the men on parade, their families in groups beside the first row of rubber trees.

Four saffron-robed monks stood before the coffins chanting from the Abhidharma, oblivious of the rain, each holding the bhusa yong, a broad ribbon attached to individual coffins.

To the uninitiated the chanting of the sutras sounded strange—low-pitched, incomprehensible. The atmosphere was heavily laden with incense and mourning. I cut a glance at Gritz standing a few feet away from me. His eyes were gimlet hard, jaw muscles bunching with emotion. A lot had happened in the last 48 hours. Taylor, Simmons and Tabouda . . . gone. Stark with one leg blown off and the other a mess . . . I glanced along the front row of inscrutable Bode faces wishing I knew the names of the four laid out before us. But they were just photographs pinned to the coffins and I felt guilty.

The don-ten wire, that was the critical piece of intelligence, I thought. There was no doubt in my mind. As sure as God made little green apples, Gritz would act on that don-ten in the jungle and as quickly as that thought flashed through my mind I could feel the clammy fist in my gut giving a tight little squeeze. It was the patrol from 361 that had started it. One of the Bodes had spotted a length of signal wire barely visible on the jungle floor. The black D10 wire—called don-ten in army parlance—meant only one thing: communications between two or more major headquarters. This was exciting stuff and by late afternoon the patrol had been reinforced with another hatchet team led by Sergeant Wallace 'Hand Job' Handwerk who was given the task of having the wire tapped. The patrol had just managed to set up the wire-tapping team with flank and rear protection deployed when darkness fell. After a sleepless night and just after dawn the following morning an enemy party sent out to check the wire sprung the 361 team and a firefight ensued. Handwerk's patrol was pinned down and taking casualties. Simmons, Taylor and eight Bodes were among those killed. The base at Tay Ninh had responded immediately and Newman, supported by gunships, took in a reaction force to relieve the beleaguered team on the ground. The reaction force linked up with the patrol after clashing with an enemy group on the LZ. In the initial contact, the Hulk killed two VC.

At about the time the 361 force was being extracted, a hatchet team from 362 to the north of the wire-tapping area came in contact with an enemy group and requested extraction. The patrol had captured a prisoner and was in the process of extraction when the chopper was hit by an RPG (rocket-propelled grenade) and machine-gun fire. With the engine damaged and two crewmen wounded, the disabled chopper flew straight into the trees. The whole thing was one unholy mess. Stark, Tabouda, the VC prisoner and three Bodes were about to load on the first slick when the RPG had gone off. Patterson, Ruiz, Hooper and Miller together with the rest of the Bodes were in the jungle providing security.

Tabouda had one small pencil-eraser sized shrapnel wound on the inside of his left thigh and appeared to be in good shape. Stark on the other hand had both legs shredded, one above the knee, the other at the shin just above the ankle. Incredibly, he had sat up, put tourniquets on both his legs, given himself a shot of morphine and dragged himself across the LZ to the other wounded. He had left a bloody trail wherever he went, tending to the wounded while the firefight was raging around him. Captain Doht, the pilot of the downed chopper, had rushed over to assist Stark, but was himself wounded in the eye. Much later I remember reading David Morrison's after-action report. He had been the reaction force team leader who went in to pull out the 362 patrol after it got into trouble. Morrison's report says:

> Everything seemed to be going OK as we listened to the patrol's radio traffic with the O1-E 'Bird Dog' aircraft with its call sign Smokey. The patrol reported that they thought someone was following them and that they had taken proper precautions of doubling back and zig-zagging on their trail. We all started

double-checking our gear as these situations usually deterio-rated quickly. As the first slick came in to pick them up, I noted that the LZ was only 75 meters wide by 150 meters long with a dog-leg in the middle, large enough to bring in one slick at a time. When our reaction team started arriving on the LZ, our chopper was taking hits. The door gunners and our team were firing above the heads of the team on the ground. They just stayed down low as we all came in firing from both doors. As I ran by I saw the wounded lying exposed in the open field of the LZ about ten feet from the wood line. We stopped about fifteen meters past them into the wood line, secured an outer perimeter while the original team loaded the dead and wounded. The gunships were raking the surrounding area with their mini-guns and rockets.

I was jolted from my musings by Gritz's voice. He was addressing the men, speaking in short sentences so that Chote, his interpreter, could translate. 'You've heard me say that sometimes we eat the bear and sometimes the bear eats us,' Gritz said and Chote, who would fit neatly under Gritz's armpit, gave the Cambodian version. 'Well, the bear sure as hell has eaten us today.' He paused, his body rigid as though he was bracing himself. I thought how apt the bear analogy was, for after all this was Rapid Fire V and Gritz had named the area of operations Bear. 'We stand here to honour the passing of our comrades who fell in battle,' Gritz went on, his eyes fixed on the row of coffins. 'And there can be no greater honour for a warrior than to die in the field of battle.' I knew that our own KIA were in the morgue at Bien Hoa in preparation to be flown back to the States. And in the Buddhist tradition the four Khmer Serei troopers would be cremated. There was a truck standing by to move them to a prepared funeral pyre at the end of the airstrip.

'Those who have fallen have done so for a righteous cause.'

There was honest conviction in Gritz's eyes as he said this, but I had doubts about the righteousness of the cause. It seemed to me that the ARVN (Army of the Republic of Vietnam) units I'd seen weren't all that keen to get to the sharp end. And the ones that were on operations seemed to be only going through the motions. So if the South Vietnamese weren't too keen to fight for their cause, what the hell were *we* doing here? I glanced around me, my eyes lighting on two of our youngest in 362— Morrison and Deo.

Morrison looked bewildered. He looked even younger than his years. In fact he reminded me of myself when I was a kid at Saint Jean D'Arc College in Shanghai. My mother had made me wear a jumper with the word 'cutie' embroidered across the chest. Well, you can imagine the effect it had on my contemporaries. One thing though, even though I was a little runt, wearing that blasted jumper forced me to learn self-defence. I knew how to throw a good combination of punches—OJT you might say—even though I scored more than my daily share of bumps and black eyes. Anyway, you'd think Morrison was just a fuzzy blond kid until you looked closely and saw the ancient eyes. 'We flew the wounded and KIA out on the first chopper. I could see Ernie Tabouda sitting up smoking a cigarette, smiling and joking as always,' Morrison had said. 'Pete Stark was out of it from loss of blood and morphine injections. We were all praying to ourselves for Pete to make it . . .' Morrison had choked up then, re-gathered himself and then added, 'We were all convinced that Ernie was OK!' En route, Ernie had just closed his eyes and gone to sleep—forever. I could see that Morrison was still in partial shock, standing at parade rest beside his patrol.

Deo was with another group of 362 Bodes close to Morrison. He was a fresh-faced kid with big hands and an infectious smile and had a softly spoken way with him. I wondered what he thought about the war. Deo came from

New York and had served a tour in Augsburg, Germany, before coming to Vietnam. He had been with a 'leg' infantry battalion of the 16th Infantry and was later assigned to the First Division—the Big Red One, LRRPs—before joining B-36. He had told me once that he had not volunteered and was simply a victim of circumstances. One thing for sure, he'd go to hell and back for Gritz. Come to think of it, all of us would.

Years later as a commanding officer of my own battalion I tried to fathom this puzzle. What persuades people to stay on a course of action despite the knowledge that it may lead to death? Why do people follow, blindly, the directions of some and not others? All I know is that Gritz affected us all in the same way. His leadership was unchallenged and let me tell you, there were a lot of hard-bitten men in that Task Force.

I glanced at Jimmy Cahill, who'd just come back from accompanying the bodies to Bien Hoa, and the trip had obviously done nothing for his morale. Newman and he had prepared the bodies for shipment to the Graves Registration Office (GRO). A recent directive required the cleaning up of the faces of those killed on the battlefield before trans-shipment—apparently GRO was having a hard time doing the job. 'I wanna meet the fool who wrote that directive,' Newman had snarled when he got back.

Cahill's tiger suit hung on him like a wet sail on a windless day. His earlier stint with Mike Force in early '67 had helped, but nothing can really prepare a person for the stuff we were doing. Sonny Edwards stood beside Cahill. He'd lost a lot of his chubbyness, but that irate look on his round mottled face persisted. He too was shaken.

Right in the middle of 361 were Bernie Newman and the Hulk. Bernie of course was an old B-36 hand, having joined the Task Force in July '67. He jealously protected his men and took what had happened personally; there was fire in his eyes. Here was this tough rooster whom you would not expect to peruse anything beyond the *Manual of Small Arms* reading poetic verses from the sensuous work of San Juan Cruz, a 17th century Spanish poet! Beside him the Hulk, too, looked angry. Newman had told me how in the beginning Gritz had contemplated cutting the Hulk from the Task Force. Having newly arrived from Fort Bragg, the Hulk had nearly pulled the helicopter out of the sky trying to climb the rope ladder during training and had blistered his hands through thick leather gloves when rappelling. That was before Operation Picnic.

I sighed, looking about me at the ragged lot of tiger suits. A Task Force parade was something I had never experienced before. There were no orders. The Bodes were silently ushered by unit while the rest of us just appeared on the airstrip at the given time, not a minute earlier or later, and found ourselves a spot. So, there was Frank 'Joe' Hillman, six two and ramrod straight, looking every inch a parade ground sergeant major. Years earlier Frank had had an accident free-falling that had left his back permanently stiff and made him look a little uppity, but that was only in appearance. Frank was one of the boys. Next to Hillman stood Jim Beatty, a wizened-up little master sergeant with military experience that went back to Korea. Beatty, the intelligence sergeant, had been recruited by Gritz from a fortified A-camp called Thien Ngon, a godforsaken shell-scarred shithole on the edge of War Zone C. Beatty had a sign printed over the doorway of his tent that said: ARTIFICIAL INTELLIGENCE IS NO MATCH FOR NATURAL STUPIDITY.

Next to Beatty was Saint Laurent, who was nicknamed Saint. The Saint never stood, he lounged, or if he wasn't lounging then he was observing you from cover somewhere. He was a natural born scout. I don't know, maybe in a previous life he was a stalker or something. Have you ever been in a situation where you think you're being observed? You look around but can't see anyone, and then finally you spot him and you *know* that the only reason you did was because *he* wanted you to see him. Actually the Saint reminded me of the Venus flytrap. But there was another side to him. Tall and ruggedly good looking with a lantern jaw that a Hollywood idol would kill for, the Saint loved women and the stories of his romantic exploits were legion. Born in Canada, André Saint Laurent had moved to California and joined the Marines, but after six years, finding life less than exciting, he had applied for duty with the Special Forces during the Cuban missile crisis. He finally got to Vietnam in '65 where he joined the Special Operations Group (SOG) after a stint with Delta. He'd been seconded to our SAS on Nui Dat hill for a short period and ribbed me mercilessly as a result of his experiences there. 'Have a cup of tea,' he'd intone with an exaggeratedly Pommy accent. Come to think of it, the Hulk used to give me shit too. He'd salute with a flourish and report good-naturedly that he was from 'the Black Watch Timex Division, Saah!'

Anyhow, Gritz had interviewed Saint Laurent with a view to getting him to join the Task Force after he'd heard about the Saint's successful mission into Laos. That was when he'd spent 30 days on his own killing people on the Ho Chi Minh trail. When I asked the Saint about his first meeting with Gritz he told me that he had queried Gritz about whether he would have to get his hair cut. 'I don't care if you have to climb a tree to take a shit as long as you teach my boys all about recon,' Gritz had said, smiling affably. The Saint had been on board the helicopter extracting Stark and Tabouda, but had escaped unscathed. I watched him as Gritz gave his peroration. He was lounging against a rubber tree, a look of unabashed adoration on his face.

I still marvel at the way we all responded with such loyalty despite the fact that all of us knew that Gritz spelt nothing but more of the same. It occurred to me that this attitude extended beyond those of us who went on the ground to include air force types like Smokey Barnes the FAC (forward air control) pilot. 'Right after the action, Major Gritz called all the new guys into the TOC for an orientation briefing,' Barnes told me. '"My name's Gritz", he says, "Commander of B-36, Special Project Rapid Fire. I will promise you two things. One, violent contact with the enemy once a week, and two, if you're porked we'll get your body out."' Barnes had shaken his head, incredulous. 'Kind of sets the tone, doesn't it?'

So what's devotion? A long time ago in Shanghai when I was a little boy I had an Amah. She was a tiny little Chinese lady. Pop had been a member of the Shanghai Volunteer Corps, a paramilitary police force whose task was to protect foreign interests in the various concessions of the international city. As the communist emergency worsened, Pop took to bringing his .38 calibre Smith & Wesson home after work. He would leave it in the drawer by the hat rack and it didn't take me long to find this hidden treasure. One evening when I thought I was alone I took the revolver out of the drawer and brandished it, much as I thought a cowboy would, at various parts of the room. I made the appropriate sounds as though I was shooting it, having a whale of a time, when suddenly I heard a shriek coming from behind me. It was Amah and she was gesturing for me to put the gun down. Though small of stature and usually quiescent by nature, she was formidable in her anger. Chastened, I put the revolver back in its place and never touched it again, but that was not the end of it. At the first opportunity, Amah rounded on Pop for his carelessness. I should explain that Amah had lost two children of her own when she was young and she tended to treat me as if I was her flesh and blood. Anyhow, she did her 'in-your-face' thing with Pop and, caught on the back foot, he mumbled something conciliatory. But she would have none of it. Half-baked appeasement would not placate her. She required an apology and a promise that any weapon brought into the house would in future be locked in the safe.

Pop capitulated, skulking off to work, and I gained a new respect that morning for a person who was prepared to risk employment to protect me. And employment was vital since her wages contributed to her family's survival. Amah lived in a small room with six other relatives in Chepei, or Pudong as it's called today. Sadly I don't think she would have survived after we were thrown out of Shanghai. As was the custom of middle-class Chinese, she had her feet bound from an early age, a cruel and painful practice that had left her feet clubbed. In another time it would have ensured her status, but it was a dead giveaway to the communist peasant army that would have made an example of her for practising bourgeois ways. She would have been shot.

I was brought back from my reverie by Gritz's voice. He was expanding his bear analogy. 'The bear has found himself a den in the jungle and he thinks he's safe in there,' Gritz snapped. You could hear a pin drop. 'Well, I promise you that nothing is further from the truth.' He glared about him. 'We will go back to his den. We will find him and we will avenge the deaths of our fallen comrades.' He paused long enough to let the interpreter translate and then raised both his arms above his head in a loose-fisted salute. 'Tay-oh,' he bellowed and the Cambodian war cry reverberated through the ranks as 400 voices chimed in.

The communications wire we'd found pointed west and I knew that that was where Gritz would go, west where the Vam Co Dong River flowed—west to the Cambodian border.

At that moment there was another chorus of voices in full throat and I cut a glance in the direction of the TOC. A chopper had just come in from the 45th MUST (Medical Unit Self Contained Transportable) hospital at Cu Chi with a load of our convalescent wounded. I could just make out Aleo,

Kovaleski and Smusch standing by the tent flap dressed in hospital blue jammies. 'The fuckers are probably AWOL,' Hillman growled, glaring at the strangely clad miscreants as the parade was dismissed and the coffins were loaded on to the back of the truck.

'Welcome back, men, that was a quick recovery,' Gritz said as he walked into the TOC.

'Oh we're doing fine, Sir,' they chorused, each showing off healing wounds. Beaming amongst them was John Wolf, still in his hospital slippers!

'What're you doing here anyway?' Gritz asked.

'They won't let us stay together,' came the response. 'So we traded our berets and Task Force patches to hitch a ride back here.'

10 PRE-DAWN REMINISCENCES

Predawn, 7 January '68.

One of the peripheral things I remember about Vietnam was sleep deprivation. It was indeed a rare occasion when the medium artillery—the one-five-fives—weren't firing harassing and interdictory missions. But on that night before the insertion on the Vam Co Dong River it was unusually quiet, a night that normally would induce peaceful slumber, a starry night with a fingernail moon low on the horizon.

Even so, I woke up in the quiet, dreading what the dawn would bring. What made it worse were the griping pains that added to my discomfort as a result of what I had eaten the evening before. Newman, Aiello, Sonny and I had visited a local restaurant in Tay Ninh and I was suffering the results of this indiscretion. While the food had tasted fine, I guess the hygiene in the place left a lot to be desired. Mangy dogs ran freely in between tables and the sticky flypaper hanging from the ceiling had long since ceased to be a trap for flies.

We had sat under a slowly grinding fan, Newman and I, discussing Ernest Hemingway's writings against a background of Oriental music that issued forth from a dusty tape recorder.

I had greatly enjoyed *The Old Man and The Sea*, finding it uplifting. I empathised with the old fisherman who wanted to catch that huge fish against all odds. I would have loved to further debate the great writer's works, but was put off by my troubled thoughts over the next day's operations.

Stumbling in the dark, I had just made it to the open-air toilet on the edge of the tarmac before nature called. Never mind the one-five-fives, the blast of gas and liquid I vented would have surely awakened the rest of the camp. I felt so embarrassed. My trousers were at half-mast, my Colt .45 resting at my feet and this reminded me of Wolf's evaluation of the weapon. I wondered how I'd go defending the Task Force Honey Pot with this cannon in the event the VC put in a surprise attack. I felt so miserable I think I would have surrendered it. Searching for soothing thoughts that would perhaps quell my rioting stomach, I thought of my childhood.

The best year of my life as a child, I've come to realise, was 1952. I say best rather than happiest because while my mother and Pop fought like cat and dog, at least we were a family. My first two years after Tubabao—which brings me to 1951—I consider as my embattled years. I tried hard to assimilate, but couldn't do anything right in the eyes of my contemporaries. I was just that tall gangly reffo kid who wore shoes while everyone else ran around bare-footed. I spoke a strange kind of English and not Strine. And I was at least a year behind in schoolwork which, my classmates decided, meant that I was as dumb as dogshit. I tried to explain to anyone who would listen that I had lost school time on a Filipino island where I did little else but perfect my marauding skills and become a marksman with the staple gun.

It was about this time that Mister George introduced me to fishing. He owned a cottage on North Stradbroke Island at a place called Dunwich and a motorboat that he kept at Wellington Point on the mainland, not far from Camp Hill.

Rumour had it that he lived on board the boat—named *Helena* after his wife—in a canal at Coorparoo when he was building his furniture factory. Even though you couldn't swing a cat in it and it stank of gasoline, I could see Mister George living in it. He was one very tough person. He led a Spartan life that revolved around his factory, only to escape to Dunwich on weekends where he would fish from daylight to dawn. Believe it or not, but that was his definition of recreation. So gruelling were his habits that he soon ran out of fishing partners. I'm sure that's the only reason a twelve-year-old kid like myself was periodically invited to join him. I lived for those occasions, not only relishing the opportunity of getting away, but enjoying the pleasure of the company of a man of simple tastes but grand character.

Anyway, my mother and Nina left the family in 1953. I greatly missed my grandmother and I had liked Nikolai, my grandfather. I could sense the tension between him and Pop, and I knew that it went beyond the squabbles at Camp Hill. Pop was almost the same age as Nikolai and, in his eyes, that made him look like a cradle snatcher. He had married my mother when she was sixteen years old. Anyhow, Nikolai had long flown the coop so that meant Pop and I were alone at Camp Hill in the downstairs flat of Mister George's house. But as I said, 1952 was my best year doing things as a family. The church played an important role in our life and in particular I recollect the Easter Sunday service at the Russian Orthodox Church in Vulture Street. I saw it recently when I was passing through Brisbane, onion domes and all. It looked run-down, a sad reminder of a different time. A time when it was the vibrant hub of the community and hundreds flocked to the services held there routinely.

The Easter Sunday service required us to catch the tram from Camp Hill to Woolloongabba, leaving a short stroll past the fire station on Main Street to Vulture Street, which in those days was a quiet leafy suburban street. Today it's a four-lane expressway. The service commenced at half past nine at night, reaching its conclusion at midnight. The Russian Orthodox Church required its congregation to remain upstanding throughout all services and the only exceptions were the very old and infirm, although the men folk often cheated by calling 'smoke-o' breaks every half hour or so. Some of them even had their hip flasks and the conversation often got quite rowdy at the back of the church where, by day, the kids were taught Sunday school. The women generally toughed it out, standing throughout the service, which says something for them, but I suppose you could argue that men are more assertive and thus took rightful liberties. Anyhow, I think the women handled the long service better.

It rained that year and I can recollect the smell of damp wool on the cool night air as we all crowded into the church. I loved the ceremony and its symbolism. I was in awe of it all, the icons of Jesus, Mary and the saints staring down upon the congregation with imploring Byzantine eyes and the bishop in his embroidered robe. I used to marvel at the deft way he would flick his brass burner held by three strands of fine gold chain at the congregation, sending little puffs of incense into the air . . . magic.

At Easter, the deacon and part of the choir used to visit households in the outlying suburbs after the main service to give blessings. The Easter of '52 was the last time together for us as a family and I remember, with some poignancy, the deacon's visit that year. Nina's best lace tablecloth adorned the dining-room table, which was laden with all sorts of dishes, the *pièces de résistance* being the koolitch—leavened sweetbread—and Paskha made with cottage cheese.

'*Khristos voskresi*—Christ has arisen,' the deacon intoned and we all responded: '*Vo instvini voskresi*—Indeed He has arisen.' Click puff, click puff went the magic incense. Oh yes,

I can recollect being caught up in the mysticism of the moment that had so awed and inspired me.

After the ceremony Pop had offered the deacon a drink and he had readily accepted. The conversation became much more animated after the deacon had consumed two or three vodkas. I also noticed that the deacon had a roving eye for attractive women. He conversed with my mother in a lively way, paying great attention to what she had to say and it occurred to me, even at that age, that the Russian clergy seemed to have a way with women. I thought of Rasputin and his enormous power as a result of the attraction the Czar's wife had for him.

I had a prick of conscience as I sat on the 'throne' on the edge of the airstrip at Tay Ninh. I had thoughts of my wife for almost every moment of every day and I guess I felt guilty that for some reason, on the eve of something I sensed could be cataclysmic, I was not with her but having flashbacks to childhood.

The thing I dreaded most was not being killed, but being taken prisoner. I knew that the Viet Cong gave no quarter to captured Special Forces and I wondered if I had the courage to take my own life if capture was imminent. Perhaps sub-consciously I had primed myself to that possibility by blocking thoughts of my wife.

11 FIRST CONTACT

January 7, 1968.

The tension is palpable. The buzz of excitement at the TOC briefings is so infectious that even Beatty has donned full battle order. Here's this bespectacled little bloke—guy, if you want the true vernacular—who would look more at home on a country porch sucking on a Bud and a corncob pipe, fretfully rousing on the team leaders as they prepare for action. The first stick of five choppers has already departed, slowly diminishing in size until they finally blur into the western haze.

On the ground, the three choppers waste no time in disembarking their passengers. Tiger suits spill from both doorways, run a few feet and drop into the tall grass of the LZ. The fourth and fifth slicks over-fly the area low and fast, the prop wash flattening the grass, sending dust and debris spinning in the backwash. The manoeuvre is designed to deceive the enemy and is timed perfectly; the first chopper on the ground, empty of its passengers, takes off smoothly behind slick number five. The other two choppers follow quickly.

It's quiet now on the LZ except for the fading sound of departing helicopters. The team rises from the tall grass and moves silently towards the line of trees. Mist hangs in tatters. It's 0800 hours, but not much sunlight penetrates the jungle canopy at the edge of the LZ only twenty yards in front of the patrol. The first mission, which was to the north-east of this location, had to be aborted because of enemy activity on the LZ. That's the reason for the late insertion.

The patrol members move like ghosts in the eerie light. There are 25 of them: Newman, Handwerk, Martin, Burr, Grant, Aleo and Lebatard together with eighteen Bodes. Their task is to recon an abandoned enemy base camp on the Vam Co Dong River. Gritz had put it another way: 'Sneaky-peak through the bushes. If you find 'em, fix 'em.' The patrol is bigger than usual and bolstered with hand-held light anti-tank weapons (LAWs) to bust bunkers. That's because of the enemy communications wire and the heavy contact two days previously. Every member of the patrol knows what's likely to be ahead of him. The wire is not very far to the east.

As they clear the LZ and enter the jungle, the patrol breaks into two files, fifteen metres apart. They head north towards the river, moving slowly, searching the ground as they go. The point man in Newman's file has just sent a field signal and Newman has stopped the patrol. He watches the Bode in front of him as he passes on the signal: one arm across the stock of his rifle, a pause and then a wave action with the free hand—water obstacle.

This is all according to plan; the patrol has reached the Vam Co Dong. The bend in the river loops to the west and the patrol changes direction to conform. Newman can hear the other file on a parallel course—the click of a rifle magazine bumping against metal, probably a harness buckle. The faint smell of sour rice makes the hairs on the back of his neck stand on end. He can't see shit for foliage, but he knows . . . He *senses* that there are a lot of folks here. Folks that are not about to spread the welcome mat . . .

The snarl of automatic weapons is so loud that it pops ear wax. The muzzles flashes are so close that Newman can feel the pressure waves bouncing off his sodden shirt. And the sound sends his heart into overdrive. As Newman hits the ground, he sees a Bode drop out of sight, as bullets smash into his body sending little puffs of dust from his clothes. There's a bunker close by. By the amount of exposed nipa palm roof, Newman can tell it's not a fighting bunker. Out of the corner of his eye he spots Handwerk firing an LAW into the bunker. There's a cloud of dust and the roof of the bunker lifts slightly.

'Let's go! Let's go!' Newman yells and, crouching, rushes forward. Aleo dumps a grenade into the disabled bunker as they rush up to it. Newman motions for Handwerk to send a search team into the bunker and Handwerk and three Bodes crawl into the narrow space below the roof which sits awry on heavy timber piles just showing above ground.

'Lookee here . . .' Handwerk signals for Martin to join him. 'One-time pads and . . . I don't know what-all.' Handwerk's voice is muffled as he dives back into the bunker.

'It's a commo bunker,' Martin yells as he too disappears inside. 'We're in the middle of a fucking headquarters!'

There are documents coming out of the ground in bundles. 'Hey Wop, get that security . . .' Newman's voice is drowned out by the sudden roar of automatic fire that rakes the area. Spurts of dirt erupt in spiky columns as broken foliage rains down on the patrol.

'Jesus . . .'

'Help me . . .'

'Medic! . . .'

It's another bunker, Newman thinks, trying hard to blot out the frantic voices. He lifts his head high enough to spot the Bode, lying prone with an LAW on his back. Newman crawls to him and tugs the anti-tank weapon off his back. The Bode makes no attempt to help. He has a hole in his head. Newman wipes the sweat out of his eyes, sights the weapon and fires, ignoring the back flash that starts a small bush behind him smouldering.

12

Newman's breath comes in long, whooping gulps. A gunship roars overhead, then banks into a tight left-hand turn, releasing 4000 rounds per minute from its mini-guns so close that he can hear the crack of the rounds striking the jungle. He'd got the radio message; 362 is on its way and Bo is talking about Mike Force being marshalled as added back-up.

Newman's got no illusions. At best his patrol will be able to absorb some punishment, but for how long? If it weren't for the fact that Bo Gritz wouldn't hesitate to commit troops into a hot LZ, his patrol would be finished in a matter of minutes. As it is, it's going to be line-ball. They had surprised a couple of VC on the edge of the LZ when they first inserted. No doubt the patrol had got the jump on them because the enemy had not expected a bunch of crazies rushing at them pell-mell through the tall grass. Newman had shot both of them in the head at close range. But now they were caught in the middle of these bunkers.

'Wildcat, Marauder, you copy, over,' Newman manages to gasp into the handpiece of his radio. He's crouched up against a tree trying to get his breath back. The rest of the patrol is in perimeter defence. Aleo, who's right next to Newman, has just been hit in the leg. He had been leaning against the same tree trunk Newman was hiding behind.

'You pigfucker, now you fucked up.' Aleo vents his anger.

'Aleo, the VC didn't shoot you because he didn't like you,' Newman snaps.

'You pigfucker . . .' Aleo ignores Newman as he rips off a full magazine on automatic.

'Now get your ass under cover before you get your head blowed off!' There's firing from the east and now they're taking automatic fire from across the river as well. Newman snatches up the handpiece of his radio. 'Wildcat, Marauder, I can hear Charlie all over the place . . . We've got bunkers . . . short of ammo, over.'

'Marauder, Wildcat. Roger. We've got some folks on the way. And an ammo resup, stand by.' Bo's voice cuts across the airwaves. Aleo is beside Newman, bandaging his leg, still cussing the VC. Martin's prone on the ground surrounded by empty magazines and discarded bandoliers. There are wounded Bodes scattered everywhere; some are stretched out near the blown-up bunkers and others, lightly wounded, are occupying spider holes in the immediate vicinity. Grant's been hit and bak si Burr is working on him, lying prone against the buttress of a tree. Burr has been hit himself.

They've got to get some troops forward, give themselves some breathing space. With Handwerk, Lebetard and six Bodes on one flank, Newman moves forward cautiously to widen his perimeter. He can hear the Cessna being flown by the forward air controller swooping down over him and he snatches up the radio's handpiece.

'Smokey Four, this is Marauder, we're going to need dustoff . . . ' The rest of his transmission is drowned out by the crackle of renewed automatic fire. Green tracer zips along at ground level. 'Holy hell . . . ' Newman can hardly hear himself.

Spotting a hole he jumps into it, his radioman on his heels. The rattle of small arms fire is punctuated by the crack of exploding B-40 rockets. His boots squelch and he turns his nose up at the awful stench. It dawns on him that in his hurry he has dived into an open trench latrine and is literally up to his knees in shit. He darts a glance to his left flank. A 66 mm LAW has just been fired at point-blank range, its muzzle flash almost touching the spider hole in front of a bunker with overhead protection.

Misfortune always comes in threes, Newman thinks. First he finds himself as a float in a Viet Cong lavatory, then the bad guys decide to renew options on their bunker system, and now he realises that the patrol is also drawing fire from the LZ! 'Which one of you motherfuckers stepped on a Chinaman?' He glares at Lebatard who's pumping rounds out of his M-16 like they were going out of style. He reaches over to his radioman and snatches the handset hooked to the front of his webbing. 'Smokey Four, this is Marauder, over.'

'Marauder, Smokey Four, I got you Lima Charlie,' the forward air controller's calm voice comes over the airwaves.

'Smokey Four, we're in heavy contact . . . taking casualties.' Holy shit . . . Newman mumbles under his breath, ducking as a B-40 rocket explodes not more than twenty feet away from him, sending clods of dirt pattering around him. 'We're going to need some help here, over.'

13 SMOKEY'S DILEMMA

One thousand feet above the ground Ken Kopke holds the Cessna O-1-E Bird Dog to a tight circle. 'Marauder this is Smokey Three, we've got some TACAIR (tactical air support) on the way. Hang in there, brother.' Kopke overlooks the minor error in call signs. The Task Force is used to dealing with Ron Barnes, but this time Barnes is the relief pilot, standing by at the FOB at Tay Ninh. As Kopke stands the little silver-gray aircraft on its wing-tip he scans the ground. Away to the east he can just see Highway 13 running north–south, a brown scar showing in patches through the jungle. Below him the Vam Co Dong River twists and turns like a snake writhing in its death throes. A clear trail points east–west, looking like an arrow pinning the snake. He leans against the windshield to get a better view, the grease pencil in his gloved hand almost touching the perspex. He'd been scribbling bearings and distances that will come in handy when the F-100s roll in. Close to a bend in the river there's a cloud of dust just starting to filter through the jungle cover and Smokey spots two gunships circling low over the smudge like pit bull terriers. This is where it's happening. This is where Marauder has just got himself involved in a shit-fight, Barnes thinks. He cuts another glance at the two gunships, noticing the little puffs of smoke from them as they fire their 20 mm cannon. B-36 had three gunships yesterday, designated a heavy-fire team, but at last light the 188th Assault Helicopter Company had pulled one of them, which meant that this morning there was only a light-fire team available for Newman down on the ground. Bo Gritz had been mightily pissed off. Three gunships allow two to remain on station while the third refuels, giving constant cover. With only two available, the time on station is severely reduced; one gunship on its own is unviable. There's going to be some ass-chewing when Gritz eventually gets to Bien Hoa, Kopke reckons: he certainly wouldn't like to be in the company commander's shoes.

Suddenly there's tracer arcing upwards and Barnes is distracted as he watches two broken green lines coming at him from across the river, crisscrossing. He jinks to keep out of harm's way. The ante has just been upped.

'Buzzard lead, this is Smokey Three, be advised there's heavy machine-gun fire coming from the north-west, over,' Kopke tells the pilot of the leading gunship. As both gunships are hugging the deck, they may not be aware of the enemy weapons. *Probably twelve point sevens*, he thinks. 'Roger, Smokey,' comes the reply amid a crackle of static. But this is only a momentary distraction. Barnes flicks through the frequencies of the three radios: VHF, UHF and FM. 'Smokey control, Smokey Three, any word on my fighters?' he asks Bien Hoa.

'Roger that, Three, you'll be getting Bobcat Five Five in ten minutes carrying Snake Eye high drags and nape plus twenty mike-mike.'

Kopke makes the calculations: Snake Eye high-drag bombs are dropped on a horizontal run from an altitude of about 60 feet. Fins deploy from the rear of the bomb and create a drag to slow the bomb's descent—that's good, greater strike accuracy.

And there are two of them for each F-100 aircraft. He scribbles '150 meters' on the windshield with his grease pencil, indicating the minimum safety distance of friendly forces from the bomb strike. The 'twenty mike-mike' of course refers to the 20 mm cannon. That's the real ace in the hole, accurate as hell . . . The napalm too is good shit, Kopke thinks.

Out of the corner of his eye Barnes spots something that makes his heart miss a beat. One of the gunships is taking hits. He can see the puffs of smoke on the craft's fuselage. The chopper flies an erratic pattern at treetop height. For a moment it's out of sight as the Bird Dog banks and then he spots it again. With a sinking feeling in his stomach, he realises that the wounded gunship is down, nose down at the southern end of the LZ, close to the jungle.

At an altitude of 500 feet Kopke stands the Cessna on its wingtip, rolls the aircraft over and dives towards the river. Through the open side windows he can clearly hear the rattle and pop of fire from the ground below. He zooms over the crashed gunship, unable to discern any movement from within . . . at least it's not burning. And then the tree line is coming at him fast. He glances at his altimeter—200 feet and winding down—the pungent smell of burnt cordite and dank jungle hits his nostrils but he's got no time to think about it, concentrating hard on flying. Okay, he can see muzzle flashes now. Shit, who're the friendlies? They're all that close to one another. 'Marauder, Smokey, tell me when I'm over the top of you,' Barnes snaps into his mike, legs working hard to correct pitch and yaw. He feels a vibration throughout the aircraft; his tail has just taken a hit.

'Smokey Four! NOW!'

'Roger.'

Jesus I'm not even going to get 50 feet clearance, let alone 150 meters! Kopke glimpses a bunker with muzzle flashes coming from it and pointing the nose of the Cessna at it, he fires one of his marker rockets. There's a rash of sparks from below his wing as the rocket releases and he's over the top of it in a flash as a plume of white smoke mushrooms from the ground. Bullseye! He pulls back on the stick and hits the throttle, lifting the nose in a steep climb. Now where's that machine-gun?

'Bobcat Five Five, Smokey Three what's your status, over,' Barnes asks, all the while his grease pencil busy on the windshield working out approach directions. The markings will serve as a crib sheet. He guides his Bird Dog further to the north, then swings east following the bend of the river. Holy shit! Down below him he can see trench lines and more bunkers. Chatter on the radio networks is intensifying as Gritz, who's flying in the C&C helicopter, calls up. 'Smokey Three, Wildcat, the cavalry's on the way.' Barnes responds automatically: 'Roger.' But he wonders whether the cavalry will be enough. What the hell have they found down there?

'Smoky Three, Bobcat Five Five, we're inbound your location ETA figures five, carrying six high drags and twenty mike-mike. Appreciate a target brief, over.'

'Roger Bobcat, friendlies are pinned down east of the river at Whiskey Tango niner niner one six four eight, white smoke marks first line of enemy bunkers. Friendlies are less than 150 metres from smoke. Repeat friendlies are *less* than 150 metres from smoke. Bomb run from north to south along the river. Hit my smoke, over.'

'Roger Smokey, I can see white smoke. Can we get the friendlies to move east . . . kinda give us some space, over.'

'Negative Bobcat. Friendly forces are pinned down at this time, over.'

'Roger.'

'Wildcat copy?'

'Roger Smokey,' Gritz responds.

'Smokey, Bobcat Five Five, okay I've got you. Okay, bomb

run north south . . .' There's a hiss of static as the jet jockey holds the squelch down momentarily. 'I'm thinking we'll have to put the high drags way the other side of the river . . .'

'Bobcat, Smokey, I'll hold two miles east. You're clear live, break break you copy Wildcat?' Barnes makes a steep turn and heads east towards his holding position while the two F-100s are doing their run. He wants to make sure that Gritz is also out of the way of the jet fighters.

'Roger that,' comes Gritz's unmistakable voice. 'Bobcat, I want you to hit that western river bank, over.'

As he cranes his neck to get a better view behind him, Kopke glimpses orange flashes as the bombs detonate and then the Bird Dog bucks, the delayed waves of concussion reaching him. Gritz's reference to the cavalry meant that the reaction force from Tay Ninh was already airborne, but will it be in time? And will it be . . . There's no time to ruminate. Kopke is on the air searching for more fighters. The trench lines are just north and east of Marauder. As he talks on the radio he does some quick calculations. He needs ordnance that can be dropped really close to the friendlies, like rockets, but he also needs some heavy stuff, and maybe napalm. The dilemma is that Marauder is right up amongst the bunkers the enemy is occupying. What's happening on the ground doesn't bear thinking about. Kopke shuts his mind to that, concentrating on marshalling the air support as he watches the second fighter zoom low over the jungle two miles to the west of him.

14 WHO'S EATING WHO?

Meanwhile, on the ground, Newman's trying to consolidate, unsure of what the hell's going on. There are Bodes going every which way, dragging their wounded. The bombing has given them the break, there's no incoming fire, just the sound of a jet swooping on them like an express train. And then there's an ear-splitting roar as the jet jockey powers away, followed by a tremendous explosion that makes the ground tremble. The pressure wave hits them, knocking some of the Bodes off their feet. Clods of dirt rain down through the trees, bigger than the size of a head. Hot metal shards spiral in the air, sizzling. And bits of branches fall, some of them bursting into flame. To the rear of him the thatched roof of a hut has started to smoulder.

Grant, who's not too badly hit, has got rear security covering their ass at the base of that hut where the wounded are, and Newman darts a glance in their direction—still there and functioning. He can see the angular shape of the M-60 machine-gun and the heads of two Bodes peeking just above the hole they're hiding in. A gunship has gone down sometime during the initial contact and two of the aircrew have survived. Somewhere near the Bodes in rear security is the pilot of the downed chopper and one of his door gunners. How those two have made it across that exposed LZ and then not been killed entering the patrol's perimeter is nothing short of miraculous. Martin appears, bare-chested. He's stooped with the added weight of a radio in a rucksack. He's carrying an M-60 as well as his own M-16. Martin looks like a demented bear and Newman can't help chuckling. A wounded bear—what would he do without this bear out there . . .

Newman spots Burr on the right flank. The medic is carrying a wounded Bode over his shoulder, dragging vines through the bush as he makes his way, crab-wise, towards him. There's a dead Bode right in front of Newman. The poor bastard bought it in the first exchange of fire. Right beside him in the hole is Newman's radioman. He's wedged himself into the moist side of the slit trench to take some weight off his legs that are disappearing into oozing muck. He smells like shit.

None of them is fooled by the lull. As the sound of the jet fighter fades into the distance a strange quiet returns to the jungle. There's the crackle of fire as the roof of the hut bursts into flame and smoke billows into the wet jungle canopy. Ten feet away, Martin is hurriedly joining extra rounds to the linked belt of M-60 ammunition. The metallic clicking sound has galvanised the Bode beside him who frantically tries to widen a spider hole by breaking away clods of dirt. Newman stacks his magazines at the front of the slit trench, noting that his ammo is running low. He grabs the handset of the radio in the rucksack beside him. 'Wildcat, this is Marauder, what's the status of the cavalry? Over.' He is surprised by the strangled sound of his own voice.

'Marauder, Wildcat, they're inbound your location at this time, ETA fifteen minutes. Hang in there, brother.'

Precious minutes. Newman glances about him as the patrol digs in. There's the chink of metal and the click of magazines being loaded. The numbers of wounded are mounting; there are four that he knows of from his patrol to add to the growing collection at the base of the hut—the one not on fire—and Newman can see at least one IV kit hung up in a tree. *It's all a matter of time*, he muses, and Gritz's words flash through his mind: *sometimes we eat the bear, and sometimes the bear eats us.* He squeezes his eyes shut. Who's going to finish up eating whom today?

15 SAINT TO THE RESCUE

TOC, Tay Ninh, 1000 hrs, 7 January '68.

There's a shell casing suspended by the entrance to the TOC with a star picket beside it. It's a casing from a 105 mm howitzer, the brass no longer shiny, and when somebody comes out of the TOC and beats the hell out of it, somewhere out there a team is in trouble. That strangely commanding sound is enough to freeze the marrow in your bones.

Edmunds the operations sergeant has just come out of the tent. He gives the shell casing a good half dozen raps, sending a wave of activity through the reaction force spread out in the shade of the rubber. Edmunds works for Crighton, who has taken over as the operations officer after being wounded at Bien Soi—Operation Picnic. Edmunds was in the 6th Marine Division during the invasion of Guam in 1944 and, along with Ritchie and Hillman, is one of the original members of the US Special Forces formed in 1952. I wonder what the hell these tough old guys eat to keep going like this!

The word is that Marauder has found the bear and he's dancing with it. And with typical Special Forces gallows humour, Edmunds exclaims that you could trust Bernie to find some crapper to dance with the bear in.

On the tarmac a chopper is warming up for take-off. The Saint squats in the corner behind the co-pilot as the chopper warms up, the backwash buffeting his face. The floor of the chopper is littered with black ammunition liners and boxes of M-16 cartridges.

There're twelve LAWs stacked on top of this mountain of explosives and the Saint casts a watchful glance at them. The LAWs, cylindrical in shape except for the pistol grip, have been removed from their carrier boxes for ease of distribution at the other end, but it makes them unstable on the flat plains and sharp angles of the crates and boxes as the chopper climbs steeply. The bare-chested loadmaster crawls over the mountain, pushing and prodding at some of the boxes. Moons of sweat stain the armpits of his green undershirt. As soon as he'd got the message that Marauder needed ammunition the Saint had made his way to the airstrip to supervise the loading. He had snatched up his M-16 on his way and he reached for it now, cradling it in his lap as the chopper banked, swinging west towards the Vam Co Dong. 'Fifteen minutes,' the voice of the loadmaster crackles in the earmuffs of the Saint's headset and he nods his assent. Below him the mat of jungle stretches on and on. He can hear the pilot and co-pilot conferring, their charts folded in their laps. Time is critical. In his mind's eye the Saint pictures Bernie and the rest of them out there and his gut rolls into a tight little fist.

There's the river! And there are smudges of smoke drifting through the jungle canopy. The pilot's communicating with Marauder, his lips forming words that the Saint can't hear; the intercom has been switched off to avoid extraneous conversation coming over the net but the Saint can make out some of the words. Now there's blue smoke billowing through a break in the canopy as the chopper swoops down towards it.

Through the towering treetops, the Saint snatches a glimpse of a thatched roof, a trail of smoke filtering upwards from its centre. A riot of images race before him: anxious upturned faces, fire, and smoke whirling in the down drafts of the flailing helicopter blades. There's not much open space ... The Saint cuts a glance at the pilot who's sitting forward in his seat, darting peripheral glances at the menacing branches that threaten to drag the chopper down. The co-pilot motions with his right hand—dump the load, we're not going to get any closer! The boxes and liners fall to the ground, spilling and bouncing on the jungle floor as the Saint and the Air Force loadmaster work frantically to deliver the load while the chopper hovers with its skids touching the tops of the trees.

'We're getting hits!' the loadmaster screams into his boom mike, but the Saint pays no heed. 'Just drop that shit down there!' he roars, shoving boxes off the floor. A crate of M-16 ammunition bounces off the skid, spilling cartridge boxes in all directions. 'Just hold the fucker steady!' the Saint yells into his mike, darting a glance at the pilot who's preoccupied with his own problems. He notices that both pilots are sitting on their folded flack jackets and can't help the smile that creases his face. *That's not where the shit's coming from* ... He cuts a glance at the chopper's ceiling, noting with concern the little puffs of dust that spring forth as bullets impact. Suddenly there's a grinding sound to the chopper's engine and the Saint can feel the floor shudder.

'Jesus Christ, we're going down!' the pilot shrieks.

16 A BOMB-HOLE AND WOLF'S MARIGOLD

1035 hrs, 7 January '68.

Five slicks loaded with part of the reaction force have just taken off and there are another five choppers coming in from the 188th Assault Helicopter Company to take the rest of us in.

Already the heat is dancing off the tarmac. The reek of aviation fuel is heavy in the air. For the umpteenth time I check my gear that lies in a pile in the shade of the rubber trees. There are 34 other piles just like it along the line of trees on the edge of the tarmac, like heaps of mastodon dung.

I heft my customised SLR. The gunsmith on SAS Hill at Nui Dat had cut six inches off the barrel, refitted the flash hider and restored the automatic switch. The rifle with a 30-round magazine was an ugly bottom-heavy bastard, but it fired a big 7.62 mm round, and on automatic it sounded like a machine-gun. Its shortened barrel also meant I could handle it better in the jungle. I had opted for the SLR rather than the M-16 and was glad I did so on my first contact. Four of the eight M-16s in the hatchet team had blockages and if it hadn't been for my ugly bastard it would have been a very much one-sided firefight.

I placed the weapon on the ground, careful not to get grime on the lightly oiled working parts, satisfied that both the stock and butt swivels were taped up with masking tape. We never carried slings. For the duration of the patrol, the rifle became an extension of your arms and the taped swivels avoided metallic noises in the jungle. Lying over the rucksack was my basic webbing. I picked it up by the harness, feeling its weight. The two pouches at the front each carried three 30-round magazines. This is where the M-16 has a distinct advantage. Both the rifle and its ammunition are considerably lighter.

Strapped to my harness I carried a smoke grenade, a field dressing, survival knife and a white phosphorus grenade. The Willie Peter, as the grenade is nicknamed, is a double-edged sword. Extremely useful in close contact, it unfortunately has a release pin without splayed ends for safety. A number of our Bodes had been barbecued by Willie Peters that had exploded when the pins had been pulled while they were pushing their way through the jungle. I check the masking tape to make sure it's firm over the pin. Clipped to the back of my harness are four water-bottle pouches, three with water bottles and the fourth with four M-26 fragmentation grenades wrapped in a sweat rag to stop them rattling.

In my rucksack I carry extra magazines, a field jacket, a strobe light for signalling purposes and two 24-hour LRRP rations. The LRRP rations come from Korea or somewhere. They're a dehydrated mixture of rice and what looks like fish heads. I don't like them because they use up too much water and make you thirsty. The last thing in my pile is a claymore mine in its shoulder-slung carrier. The claymore has been adapted so that it can be used as a throw-down. If you have to break contact in a hurry it can be tossed behind you, and when the initiating wire is unrolled and pulled, it jerks into a more or less aligned position facing the enemy. You press the clacker . . . boom! Hopefully you've bought yourself some time.

The little comfort items such as a poncho, groundsheet and blankets are missing, I've replaced them with extra ammunition. The weight of my gear is formidable. I'm thankful that I'm six four and can manage to carry it even though I feel like a mule. There are days when I convince myself that I should opt for an M-16, but then I remember those Bodes thrashing around trying to clear stoppages while bits of bark were being stripped off the trees around them.

The taxiway, refuelling point and safety bays for the choppers are all empty. Gritz is up in the C&C, I heard him earlier on the air, talking to Smokey and Marauder. Something had gone wrong but at the time I didn't know about the debacle that was being played out in the air. In his book *Called To Serve*, Gritz describes it this way:

> The target area was easy to define; it ran along the Oriental River just inside Vietnam—across the river was Cambodia. The assault teams orbited a safe distance to the north in a trail of UH-1Ds. We were in commo with the invisible high-flying Stratofortresses, having flown 3,000 miles from Andersen Air Force Base at Guam at an altitude of 35,000 feet using LORAN and radar navigation. At exactly the prescribed time they released their carpet of bombs. I waited to see the matted jungle erupt as the 750 pound bombs carpeted an area one kilometer wide by two kilometers long. With that kind of coverage, how could they miss? Shock waves moved along the ground as each B-52 dropped its 54,000 pounds of ordnance, but not on the target—the strike was five miles off target inside Vietnam! I screamed into the radio on the UHF frequency assigned to the ALO coordinating the strike: 'What the hell is going on! They're dropping the bombs way off target!' The calm voice of the staff officer came back explaining that 'regulations prevented bombing any closer than five miles to the border, therefore the USAF had put the bombs as close as

rules of engagement would allow. It was regrettable that we weren't informed.' I went berserk, but there was nothing that could be done. The B-52s dutifully emptied their bomb bays and returned back to base, their mission accomplished.

I wondered if we'd see Gritz on the ground before the end of the day. I had this ominous feeling that today was the day. There was no doubt in anybody's mind that if push came to shove and the reaction force was threatened with annihilation, Gritz would order his C&C chopper to land where he could get to the last of his troops. He wouldn't hesitate to die in place, magazines stacked in some shithole out there. That ominous thought reminded me of Frank Hillman's story.

That same day that Smusch had his 'instant replay' and Ron Grey did the foxtrot round the old bare tree and got plucked by the C&C chopper, Hillman comes up with his story. 'It's the middle of the night. There's one hell of a storm in progress and Pride's in deep shit in the boonies,' says Hillman.

'Where's Dirty Ernie?' Gritz grumbles, having been woken out of a deep sleep by Ritchie who was dripping rain all over him. Dirty Ernie Snider, who commanded 361 at the time, pipes up, 'I'm right here, Sir, stand'n in the rain behind Cap'n Ritchie. If he'll move over I think maybe we can all get in out of the weather.'

Fully awake now, Gritz turns to Snider. 'What do you think?'

Snider's shedding water like a swamp mallard. 'Sir, Pride's jumpy, but he wouldn't call for extraction unless it was life or death. You know he hates flying at night, particularly in this weather. If there's any way, I say we try and get him,' he says.

'Get the aircrew up. We're goin'. We'll take the C&C and two gunships. Frank, get the TOC on full alert,' Gritz snaps.

'Bo, I don't think the pilots will fly under these conditions,' says Ritchie.

'Who's *askin'* them, Ritchie? Just get the flight leaders into the TOC.'

SHADOWS ON THE WALL

Hillman gets that pensive look and a smile touches his lips. 'Anyhow we're in the air. It's black and the rain's coming at us on the horizontal.'

Suddenly the radio crackles: 'Wildcat, Wildcat, this is Apache One, I can hear a chopper. Come more to your right, more to your right, over.'

Gritz has that determined look. 'Apache One, Wildcat. We're comin'. What's your current position?'

There's static on the radio and then with an almost incoherent rush, 'Sir, Charlie's all over us! We've circled wagons in a bomb hole full of water. We're out of ammo. There's heavy movement all around us. If you don't come in now it's over for us!'

Gritz's got that fuck-you look. 'This is Wildcat, Roger. Use your pen-flares to send up a red cluster. Keep giving directions until we have you. Once the gunships are overhead, use your strobe light to pinpoint the friendlies. The guns'll orbit until we can get a slick down to you, over.'

What slick? Hillman wonders. There's only the C&C. Surely . . .

'Well, there's one helluva fight going on down there,' Hillman recounts. 'Green and red tracer every which way you look and the gunships are circling below us. I see Bo leaning half out the door. "We'll have to try and get the teams out with the C&C," he says. "We can't do that!" roars the flight commander. I can see his crazy eyes in the eerie light cast by the instrument panel,' says Hillman. '"It's too much weight. We can't hold 'em all even if we can get down through all that fire. No. We won't do it!"' Ritchie and I exchange glances. I put my arm around the pilot and calmly ask him to do what Major Gritz ordered. The captain just sits there with an expression of horror on his face and I notice that it's the young warrant officer who's flying now, the flight commander has turned the controls loose and is clutching his armoured seat plate. The young guy didn't blink an eyelid, he just flew the

104

damn thing.' The stress is clearly cameoed on Hillman's face as he draws on his recollections. 'The pilot turns on the landing light which looks like a solid beam in the rain and there's a bomb hole below us surrounded by jungle. People are shooting at us . . . It's like I'm on some kinda LSD trip . . . Jesus . . . Bo's yelling for the pilot to put the skids under water so the men could climb aboard . . . everybody's shooting . . . We're hauling our men on board and I don't have to be a pilot to know that we're overloaded to hell.' Hillman pauses.

'"Let's go", says Gritz, but every time the chopper tries to lift, it wallows. I can hear the snick, snick as the blades bite into the jungle canopy. "We've got to lighten the load", Bo says, and grabs Pride by the shoulders. The major has ripped his flight helmet off and it's plain that he means to jump off with Pride. I tell you, Pride's got that "you've got to be kidding" look.' Hillman's brows knit into a thoughtful expression. 'You know how a bumblebee's not supposed to be able to fly, but it does? Well, that's how it was with that chopper of ours. It wasn't supposed to fly. But it did. It groaned and rattled and roared and . . . Jesus . . . it broke away from that goddamned bomb hole and we were flying. We were crying and laughing and looking at each other as though we'd never seen each other before.'

I say a quick prayer that we don't have a replay of the bomb hole incident. I really don't want to see Bo Gritz in the same circumstances on the Vam Co Dong River, but if it were to happen then this is the family with whom I would be sharing that experience. I looked around me. I was thinking of them as family yet it occurred to me that I didn't really know them all that well. I glanced around at the team making ready to depart. Even as that thought registered, another found its way into my mind. I had recently spoken to Handwerk about the strangeness I felt in being involved in life and death situations while not knowing well the people around me. Handwerk's response had buoyed me considerably. 'When you're on the ground and taking fire and the other team's in trouble and there's only enough air to lift one of you out, you've got to make the right call,' Handwerk had said. 'And that call's got nothing to do with *knowing* people. It's got *everything* to do with being brothers.' Handwerk had selflessly refused to be extracted under fire when Spencer's team was in trouble, availing Spencer the use of the air. Spencer felt bad about getting extracted while Handwerk had been left to evade the enemy during the night and it wasn't until 1988 at a B-36 reunion that Spencer was able to talk to Handwerk about it.

'Dave,' Handwerk had said. 'We were in trouble, but your tem was going to get killed. It was our choice, and it was the right one.' After looking at Spencer for a long moment, Handwerk had added, 'You would have done the same for me.'

Anyway, here I was hurriedly forming up. Panzica was in the rubber trees rummaging around a crate of claymores, loading himself up with more. I didn't know Panzica at all. He was in animated conversation with a group of Bodes, his close-cropped head shining in the sunlight beaming through the trees.

Then there's Ruiz—as in *Grease*. He's an LRRP who by origin is Hispanic. Dark hair, dark eyes and a flashing smile. I must admit I can't work him out. He's a good soldier, but has a cruel streak in him. We'd come in from a patrol one day and the crotch of my tiger suit pants had torn. I remember Ruiz rushing to his tent for a camera. I don't know, maybe I'm just embarrassed at having my weenie photographed.

Sonny Edwards is not far from Ruiz. He's squatting beside his gear, wiping his florid face with a sweatrag dangling around his neck. It seems his brows are constantly knit into a frown. He's pernickety about everything being just right and I guess this crazy Yankee outfit may get on his goat at times. Sonny's been with me on almost every patrol and he's feeling the strain same as I am. A Sandgroper from Subiaco in Perth, Sonny had been on the state railways until '58 when he got called up for

National Service. I guess the fact that his last posting before Vietnam was with One Commando Company, a part-time soldier's outfit, contributed to his attitude. Sonny's good value in the field and I'm glad of his presence.

Pak has two fingers missing on his right hand—the second and third—leaving the index and little fingers to do the job. He's lost them in an accident with a time-pencil a few months ago. Pak's my Bode radioman and bodyguard. He's carrying an over-and-under—an M-79 grenade launcher and M-16 combination—which he cradles in his arms like a shotgun. The radio strapped to his rucksack makes him walk with a forward lean. I'm constantly amazed at how these small-framed people can handle the weight so adroitly. Pak is always beside me; he's my shadow and I live in admiration of him. I can't imagine the willpower it must have taken to come back after blowing up his hand, but there he is. Someone once told me that Pak has been earmarked to command a Free Khmer battalion if he survives. His stint in Special Forces is simply training for the coming war in Cambodia. Boy, what a life.

Thinking of the walking wounded reminds me of that other bloke, John Wolf. Wolf slips his shirt off and mops the sweat off his glistening shoulders. He's lost a lot of weight, looks as skinny as a drover's dog. His tiger suit pants hang bunched on bony hips, fastened in place by green nylon cord. The still-healing scar from his gunshot wound is visible, a purple cicatrice in the shape of a marigold low on his abdomen. *When there was a blue tinge I just sewed them up . . .* The words flashed through my mind. Pop's dining room in the flat at Camp Hill . . . a table laden with piroshki, cold meat and a plate of salted herring with onion rings and slices of hard-boiled egg. There's a bottle of chilled vodka on the table and beads of condensation form on it. It's Zubrovka—Bison Weed—vodka, arguably the best on the market. Pop didn't have much money but he loved to entertain, and on Saturday nights in the early fifties some of his cronies would gather to eat good food, drink the best that was around and swap treasured yarns. One of his regular guests was Doctor Nathing, an imposing man in his mid-sixties with silver grey hair. Doctor Nathing's puffy eyes were a legacy of hard living. He had been a surgeon during the advance on Habarovsk in 1921 when the Siberian winter had stopped the White Russian army in its tracks. Of course I was too young to be in on the conversation, but I'd hover about listening to what was being said, and Pop tolerated my presence so long as I wasn't intrusive. In any case, with a few shots under the belt he was magnanimous.

'At least during Habarovsk we were fortunate enough to have a medical facility, eh doctor?' Pop had said as he refreshed Doctor Nathing's vodka glass.

'You're referring to the hospital train of course, my dear Yevgeni Mikhailavitch.' Nathing's smile was full of irony. Pop had offered the surgeon a steaming plate of fish pies and Nathing inclined his leonine head, obviously relishing the aroma. '*Spasiba*, my friend.' He heaped the pies on his plate. 'They made much of that train, all good propaganda.' He bit into a pie, dabbing his mouth with a napkin, then returned to the matter being discussed. 'You never had the misfortune of being on it?' He glanced at Pop.

'No. I was never on it,' Pop had said.

'Ah, that's a good thing. You know in the end we had no morphine.' The doctor made a deprecatory gesture. 'We didn't even have peroxide to cleanse the wounds properly. There were wounded everywhere, even in the passageways. I'd open them up and if there was a blue tinge to the gut I'd just sew them back up and the sanitaar would push them into a far corner to die.'

While it was Wolf's scar and the association of colours that had triggered my memory, it occurred to me just how pointless all this was. So strong was Wolf's sense of duty that he felt compelled, but I couldn't understand what the hell he was doing lining up to jump on board the next bunch of slicks to head for the Vam Co Dong River when he should have been in rehab. Wolf has put his shirt back on and has thrown his harness over his shoulders, wincing as he does so, but I've got no time to ponder this. There's a sound of approaching helicopters and I squint into the sun as the five choppers drop towards us, the down draft kicking up a storm of dust. I shrug into my gear, dread squeezing my gut. My legs feel like lead. It's time to go.

17 SAINT AND THE JOLLY GREEN FROG

1100 hrs, 7 January '68.

The re-supply chopper lurches violently, but the Saint is too busy kicking out the last of the boxes to pay attention. The floor tips upward . . . blue sky. There's stuff sliding all over the floor, boxes and all sorts of gear ricocheting around . . . The engine sounds like it's crunching up nuts and bolts. The Saint rips his headset off and now he can hear the long bursts of incoming machine-gun fire.

Tak tak . . . taktaktaktak . . .

'I'm gonna fly 'er down! . . . Control spin!' the pilot yells, spittle spraying from his lips. The Saint can make out the words even though his headset is in his lap. *I'm going down and . . .*

The trees slant at a crazy angle, then there's a patch of blue sky, then trees again . . .

. . . all I've got is . . .

The noise from the engine changes to a grinding shriek. Tops of trees race towards them . . .

. . . one miserable magazine . . .

The Saint snatches a glance at his M-16, painfully aware

that in his rush to board the chopper he had neglected to bring his webbing! *Jesus Christ, how could I have done that!* But more immediate things press on him. He grabs at the stanchion beside him as the chopper shudders, almost losing the M-16 as it slides towards the open door. Trees loom large and he clamps his eyes shut, anticipating the impact as the chopper spins away, its main rotor shearing branches in its path. And then as if by miracle the chopper clears the treetops and they're heading towards the LZ, rotating slowly while the engine continues to groan and grind. With a violent bang that sends stars exploding before his eyes, the skids bump the ground once, twice, and finally the chopper comes to a halt about 30 feet from the edge of the jungle.

The Saint clambers out on shaky legs. He wipes away a smear of blood from his cheek that tastes coppery. A quick check confirms that he's not badly hurt, and neither are the two pilots who scamper out of the chopper. The last one to crawl out of the door hatch is the loadmaster, blood trickling from a head wound. The chopper is making weird metallic groaning noises but there's no fire. The pilot and co-pilot look uninterested, as if they've abrogated all responsibility now that they're on the ground; the Saint spots one of them sitting on a termite's nest, a dazed expression on his ashen face. 'Get down!' he growls, waving the pilot off his perch. The pilot jumps as if woken from a deep sleep and awkwardly assumes the prone position in the tall grass. His co-pilot follows suit. Both carry .45 automatic pistols that are still holstered by their sides. Oh boy . . .

It turns out that the loadmaster's head wound looks worse than it is. 'My old lady beats up on me more'n that,' he says and spits in the grass. He had bumped his forehead when the chopper had gone into rotation and the cut bled profusely. In the face of their predicament the Saint is buoyed by the man's feisty attitude and the AR-15 in his lap.

A cold douche of small-arms fire snaps the Saint back. A whiff of cordite drifts from the jungle as the firing increases, raw and sharp against the foetid smell of vegetation. He cuts a glance at the pilot, automatically ready to defer decision-making to the officer. Not that the Saint can't make decisions. On the contrary, he has spent most of his army life making them for himself and his patrol. But essentially he's a loner and if he had a choice he'd simply melt into the jungle and slowly, quietly make his way back to either Suoi Da at the base of the Black Virgin Mountain or Tien Nghon. He had no doubts that he could find one of the two Special Forces camps within four or five days. The thought reminded him of the 24 hours he had spent surrounded by a platoon of NVA soldiers near the tri-border in Laos.

About ten days into his stint in Laos, the Saint had found this saddle-shaped feature running off a sharp ridgeline and had instantly sensed that this was a place where travellers would rest, welcoming a break from the hard going. A cursory check had showed cut saplings and machete marks—this place had been used as a way-station. It was an hour before last light. Normally he would have made for a patch of bamboo for the night, knowing that any enemy patrols would keep away because of the way the stalks creaked and popped, even in the smallest breeze. But this was too good to pass up. He decided to set up an ambush in the hope that if he was in luck and a small enemy party moved into the way-station through the night he just might be able to kill one or two of them at first light with his silenced sniper's rifle.

Just on last light a party of ten NVA soldiers moved in and set up their hammocks. An hour or so later, another fifteen or so soldiers arrived, their flashlights twinkling in the dark. By midnight another party of five or six had arrived. The Saint found himself in the middle of a camp with small cooking fires and folks in hammocks all around him! He spent the night sitting transfixed, his scrim net over his face and shoulders, not daring to breathe. And to make matters worse, the enemy seemed in no hurry to move at first light. It was early afternoon before he managed to get away and find a place to rest up.

The Saint is brought sharply back to the present by the sound of a sharp explosion. A rocket grenade has gone off somewhere in the jungle close to Marauder. The pilot lies next to his ants' nest, darting fearful glances behind him at the tree line. The co-pilot is not even visible in the tall grass. Neither of them is about to volunteer for *this* piece of leadership training—no way. What to do? Options are limited. The Saint has to protect the chopper with its radios, maps and signals material. In the worse case, they would have to burn the chopper, and to this end he clambers aboard, scanning the debris scattered across the metal floor. He picks up three cardboard boxes of M-16 ammunition and shoves them down the front of his shirt, opens another one and removes four tracer bullets, feeding them into his magazine. He'll use the tracer to set off the fuel if needs be.

Escape and evasion is not an option. Not for four men. The party would not survive 24 hours out here without being found and captured. If he's got to trash the chopper then his best bet would be to link with Marauder, *and that's not going to be easy*, the Saint thinks as the firing intensifies.

The *wop wop* sound of an Iroquois helicopter is unmistakable, and as the Saint looks up he sees the chopper flaring as it drops towards them. It's unbelievable! In the midst of this carnage, unscathed and pristine comes this jolly green frog! He bundles the crew aboard and points to the wrecked chopper resting nose down no more than twenty feet away. Forming a moue with his lips, he mouths 'boom', indicating that he wants to blow up the wrecked aircraft, but the door gunner shakes his head, vigorously waving him aboard.

This is Rapid Fire, the Saint muses. *This is the crazy,*

unpredictable yet somehow loveable thing about Rapid Fire, casualties and all . . . He shuts his eyes, resting back against the frame of the helicopter, his thoughts on that day when . . . when his whole patrol got hit—Rico, Newman, Teevans, Spahn, the four Bodes . . . Jesus, he'd gladly give back the Silver Star they gave him for that action to have Teevens back. Saint Laurent can feel his tear ducts welling. He's glad of the slipstream whipping past his face, blowing away the tears that come readily. He'll never forget that morning . . . November 17 . . . Yankee Tango zero two three three zero seven. They'd heard the wood chopping and moved up in file, straight into the base camp . . . Spahn got hit and Teevens, the medic, had gone in to get him. And then Teevens was hit in the back of the head and . . . and the Saint and Johnson went forward to recover Teevens' body.

The thing that was unforgettable was the way Teevens had Spahn between his legs. Out there with B-40 rockets and automatic fire going off, Teevens, with his back to the enemy, was covering Spahn with his own body as he tried to drag him back. He had slumped once when he was hit, recovered and continued to drag Spahn before being hit again and this time staying down. Bernie Newman had set up a claymore with a Willie Peter in front of it and the Saint had ordered them all to fall back with the wounded. Shit, they were all wounded . . . dragging and pulling each other through the Jay while he crouched and waited and listened as the bastards came . . . Bang! And he was moving, diddy-bopping out of there, dragging his wounded leg, emptying magazines as he went . . . Yeah. He'd give up his Silver Star just to have Teevens back, and Lynn Jnr, and Larry Williams who went in a few days later, into that godforsaken base camp . . . What price a Silver Star? Saint felt the lump growing in his throat, his chest feeling as though someone the size of the Hulk had sat his ass on it . . .

Yeah, they'll send a Chinook out to recover that chopper, the Saint thinks. They'll send a Chinook after the Task Force porks the best part of a goddamn regiment of those folks out there. Tears run freely now as he leans back against the pilot's seat with the wind swirling around him and the chopper gains height rapidly. Yeah. This is Rapid Fire.

18 DEO AND THE LEGION OF SMILING FACES

DEO AND THE LEGION
OF SMILING FACES

1100 hrs, 7 January '68.

Deo cuts a glance at Bradley, who has pulled a compass attached to a nylon cord around his neck. He catches a glimpse of a muddy river through the foliage. Along with a dank marsh smell there's a distinct odour of unwashed bodies and urine—beaucoup VC. On the LZ, the first elements of the 362 reaction force climb to their feet and move to the north towards the sound of firing. They haven't gone more than 75 metres when the Bode in front of Deo stops so suddenly that he bumps into his back. Ahead of him in the jungle half-light Deo spots a figure dressed in a khaki uniform, no more than fifteen feet away. In a reflex action he points his M-16 and fires a short burst from the hip. Stung by the sudden firing the patrol rushes forward dragging vines and torn branches, firing as they go.

'We've got bunkers,' somebody yells but Deo can't see a thing. As he cuts a glance at the towering trees above him, he notices that the upper branches have been bent and tied to form a continuous cover through which virtually no sunshine penetrates.

Deo's on the left flank but he might as well be on the moon.

There are branches and clods of dirt flying everywhere and all he can hear are firecrackers going off right over his head. He yells at Martin, but there's no way he can be heard. *What the hell am I doing here?* His mind is reeling. He hadn't even volunteered for LRRPs, let alone this crazy outfit! He had joined the army at seventeen, serving at Fort Wainwright before completing a tour in Germany. *This shit's alright for the hard core*... Let's face it, he couldn't even bring himself to call Martin the Hulk. Well, he may have snuck in the odd Wop when referring to Aleo, but not the legends of the Task Force. Never.

Just keep your head down. Hide. Sound thinking, after all there's a shitstorm out there and... *and I'm not even SF. Just a poor kid from Troy, New York. One of Missus Deo's ten children is all.* Deo shuts his eyes and burrows down in the muddy earth that smells of rotting vegetation. *You know, maybe, just maybe the VC might miss me in this little hole I've dug for myself.* Yeah, if he can sit this out a reaction force is bound to get here sooner or later and save him. And then he thinks of Stark, the way the medic crawled around on the stumps of his legs tending to the other wounded. And Tabouda and... *Jesus Christ, what the hell am I doing here?* He lifts himself out of the mud and, crouching behind a tree, lets go half a magazine at the twinkling red flashes that flicker out of the gloom. He jinks in the direction of the patrol, rushing forward a few steps and then firing, heading towards the sound of returning fire. Out of the corner of his eye he spots the Bodes who are with him on flank security, also moving forward. On the periphery of his vision he sees one of them fall, then another. But there's no time... There are Bodes down everywhere and he spots Martin hunched over, trying to drag someone along the ground. The crotch of his pants is torn and there's blood all over the front of his shirt.

Deo hears the sound of a whistle, and another further to the right. *Fuck! Reinforcements* . . . Apart from the first VC they'd surprised, all the other firing has been from spider holes. He hasn't seen a single enemy . . . seen muzzle flashes though. But this is different. This is . . . *Holy shit!* They're coming, like ghouls in the night. Men in khaki uniforms, some with pith helmets, moving swiftly towards them through the jungle. 'Pull in tight,' Deo yells, but no one can hear him in the din. In any case they're moving towards him now, Martin looking just like the Incredible Hulk—weird; the Wop crabbing sideways, dragging a leg, trousers half blown off and saturated in blood. Here comes Bradley. He's carrying a Bode in a fireman's grip over his shoulder. There's so much blood over both of them that Deo can't make out whether Bradley's been hit as well. *Okay. Here comes Missus Deo's little boy Richard. Here comes the little snot-nosed kid from Troy. Fuck you!* Deo rests the stock of his M-16 against a moss-covered tree stump, takes deliberate aim and fires a sustained burst, sweeping the barrel along the line of approaching enemy. *Fuck you!* White-hot rage engulfs him. *I fear . . . I fear no evil.*

The breech clicks empty and he reverses magazines, cocks the M-16 and fires again, and again, choosing random targets. *Plenty of motherfucking targets to choose from!* As he lays down the fire the rest of them move in: Martin, the Wop, Bradley and what's left of the Bodes—hauling ass. *Steady. You'll run out of ammo.* Deo switches to single shots, scrabbling in his pouches to find more magazines.

Something punches him in the side and he's down. Incredulous, he glimpses the small tear in his shirt and the spreading red blossom. He's been hit. Splinters fly as bullets impact into the tree stump beside him. He sits up, sights his M-16 and fires, heartened by the fact that Martin beside him is also firing. He feels a buzzing sensation in his shoulder and realises that he has just been hit again.

Dizzy . . .

Somehow the sound of battle has lost its staccato sharpness. He feels a strange euphoria. *You walk the walk and talk the talk* . . . the thought echoes in the chambers of his mind. What's that all about? *Oh yes.* Deo looks up and in the smoke of burnt cordite he sees the legion of smiling faces: Sergeant Snorkle, the Hulk, the Saint, Dirty Ernie, the Amazing Spiderman and a few others whose features are blurred. But this thing isn't over yet. He leans forward to snatch a fresh magazine from a pile that has spilled from his basic pouch, but the pit he leans into seems bottomless and very, very dark.

Time to rest a minute. Time to . . .

19   ROLLING-STONE ALLEY AND THE JACK-IN-THE-BOX

1120 hrs, 7 January '68.

'Two minutes,' the crew chief yells. He pokes two fingers in front of my face and I nod in response. My stomach lurches as the chopper tilts and begins its steep descent. A river bend swings into view momentarily, muddy water flowing beneath towering trees that crowd the banks. Then there's jungle, thick secondary forest close to the river. As the chopper flattens out there's a large expanse of open ground that's coming at us fast. There are seven of us crowded on the floor in a tangle of rucksacks and weapons. Like all Iroquois troop carriers in Vietnam, this one has had its sliding doors removed and the webbed seats slotted back to maximise on space. I cast a glance at the door gunner, an African-American who wears a flack jacket over his bare shoulders, increasing his size to enormous proportions. A steel helmet covered with faded scrim tops his head. The gunner swings his M-60 on its pintle mount in a dry run as we flatten out at treetop height and begin our run-in. The chopper's on loan to us for the operation and I don't recognise any of the crew.

As we skim the ground the gunner fires long bursts, spent brass casings fluttering behind us like confetti in the slipstream. Some of the brass drops within the chopper, tinkling and rolling in little smoking heaps around us. I cut a glance at Sonny, who sits resolutely beside his rucksack, his M-16 in his hands. He looks back at me with a blank expression and I give him a thumbs-up to which he responds with a nod. This is no time for words, either of comfort or encouragement. The Bodes are packed in around us. Without exception they wear a miniature Buddha around their necks and, cued by the door gunner's yammering M-60, each one of them has placed his sacred relic in his mouth. The Bodes believe that should they die, the close presence of Buddha guarantees them entry to Nibanna. The Yanks have a quaint expression for it: popping the Buddha.

The chopper's skids touch the ground momentarily and we pile out to the accompaniment of the M-60 that seems to be going berserk, smoke rising from its barrel, tracer zipping on our flank. And then I'm running for the tree line, stumbling over termite nests, slowed down by the high grass. Out of the corner of my eye I spot other groups doing the same as the choppers deliver their loads.

Close to the tree line on my left a gunship is firing. The sound of its mini-guns is like calico tearing. *Praaap,* and then again, and again there's that sound as the second gunship joins in. *Praaap praaap papapraaap . . .*

Almost at the tree line . . . out of breath . . . lungs burning, windpipe crackling, I snatch a glimpse at an F-100 zooming down to treetop height along the line of the river—backswept wings with a sandy brown superstructure and swirls of grey and green camouflage paint. White smoke traces a path from its undercarriage as it fires its rockets. The radio is a constant crackle of transmissions but I pay it little heed. The thing that preoccupies me is the rattle and pop of small-arms fire away to my left. We'd been inserted to the right of Marauder and my job is to swing west and head for the river. Head for the sound of firing.

At the edge of the jungle I take a compass bearing—azimuth reading in Yankee parlance—and we set sail through the thick foliage. Effectively we're an over-strength platoon, but there's more coming and I'm buoyed by that thought. It's not bad going underfoot and we make good progress when suddenly the sound of firing has me flat on the ground. The rabbit in my chest is doing inverted somersaults and I can hear the pulse in my throat. I'm lying in what looks like the dry bed of a small soak. There are smooth river stones and . . . *a rolling stone gathers no moss.* The asinine thought pops into my head and I swear at myself for thinking silly thoughts in the midst of a crisis. I can hear the Bodes shouting to each other in high-pitched voices. A long time ago a large tree had fallen and a sizable branch now rests over the soak. I crane my neck to scan the ground in the triangle made between the soak and the branch. I see shit. Nothing but dripping leaves and those rolling stones that gather no moss. And . . .

Pangapangapangapanga . . .

The unmistakable sound of an AK-47 is so loud it causes my ears to block. I duck my head, tasting dirt. The smell of rotting vegetation is in my nostrils. And down the tunnel of the soak, like pebbles down a chute, comes a tinkling shower of little brass casings. One of the smoking casings bounces off my nose and I stare at it, cross-eyed. There's no mistaking it—7.62 mm short. For what seems an interminable period I remain frozen to the ground, eyes shut, with this bizarre feeling that if I look up rolling-stone alley and the little brass tunnel I'm going to see the muzzle of that AK-47 staring at me like a dark accusing eye. At that moment I recollect Pop's words: 'You know the difference between courage and cowardice, son?' Of course I didn't, and in any case I couldn't have cared less at the time. I was in my early teens and preoccupied with girls. Pop and I had been sitting in the kitchen in the small hours after one of his Saturday night soirées. His guests had left and we were surrounded by dirty dishes and empty bottles. 'A hair's breadth,' he'd said. I hadn't paid much attention so I asked him what he was talking about. 'The difference is a hair's breadth.' He'd drunk a fair bit so I put his comments down to his general maudlin state. But right now I can understand what he had been driving at. At this moment lying in the soak with an unknown enemy taking random potshots at us, it takes a lot of effort on my part to simply move my head a little in order to see . . .

. . . Nothing. Just dripping leaves, river stones and . . . little brass spent cartridge shells. There's the occasional pop of small-arms fire and voices raised in urgency. One voice persists, a Bode voice calling out: 'Dai hui . . . ooof . . .'

Ooof? What the hell's that?

'Dai hui . . . ooof . . .'

I crane my neck to get a better look but there's nothing to see, just a triangular aperture . . . leaves and . . .

A bunch of leaves at the end of a branch has moved sideways. I blink to clear my vision, disbelieving the evidence before my eyes. From behind the bunch of leaves comes the barrel of an AK-47 as perpendicular as a flagpole, and following that, a head. The head's side-on to me, no more than three feet away. I can clearly see a mop of oily black hair. Mesmerised, I watch the flagpole tip to the horizontal and then . . .

Pangapangapanga.

. . . And then the little brass casings tinkle and tumble past the rolling stones that gather no moss. As quickly as it appears, the Jack-in-the-box is down, but in the reverse order: oily hair, then the flagpole to the perpendicular, periscope down, then the bunch of leaves fixed to what looks like a wicker basket lid pulled by a cord of some kind. Once the lid slides into place there's no sign of the Jack-in-the-box. I can't believe my eyes!

SHADOWS ON THE WALL

My rifle is pinned under my chest after my sudden dive into the soak and as I inch it forward, taking the weight on one elbow and off my basic webbing, my eyes are riveted to the spot where Jack-in-the-box had disappeared. At any moment I expect him to reappear and the thought of eyeballing the muzzle of that AK-47 freezes the marrow in my bones. Every fibre in my body screams at me to hurry, but I know that if I make a noise I may well pre-empt the sniper's actions before I'm ready. So I move slowly, inwardly cursing every time some jutting metal part of the rifle gets caught on my webbing, slowing down the process. I have this perverse feeling that Jack-in-the-box is aware of what I'm doing and is simply waiting for me to get my weapon sufficiently forward to give me a glimmer of hope before popping out of the ground and . . . Cold sweat trickles down the back of my neck. I can still hear the Bode somewhere just in front of me calling out, 'Dai hui, ooof . . . oof . . .' but I'm focused on shooting the Jack-in-the-box before he blows my brains out. A rill of sweat runs down my left cheek, then splatters on the wooden stock of my rifle—three little blooms as the rifle inexorably moves forward. *How come the bastard hasn't popped out yet?* My hands are shaking. If it were not for the fact that I'm attempting to shoot him at point blank range I wouldn't have the confidence of hitting the target. With my hands the way they are I couldn't hit a barn door with a shotgun at ten paces.

And then it all happens with a rush. I stick the muzzle of my rifle plumb in the middle of that bloody bush and let go four rounds in quick succession. Pak is beside me. I hadn't noticed his approach, but now he joins me, firing a burst of M-16 from his over-and-under. The impact of the bullets has shattered the wicker lid and the hole is exposed. Jack-in-the-box will never perform his trick again.

From my upright position I can see that the soak peters out into a shallow crawl trench and there are numerous other spider holes visible, but only if you take particular care to look. Beyond the crawl trench I spot the Bode who was calling out, and the instant I spot him I understand what it is that he was trying to say. Crumpled on the ground less than ten feet away is John Wolf, and crouched beside him is bak si Thanh with his paramedic's bag open and shell dressings all over the place. Thanh has cut one of Wolf's trouser legs to expose his wounds. The Bode had been yelling out, 'Dai hui . . . WOLF!' Trying to attract my attention to the fact that Wolf had been hit. And indeed Wolf looks in bad shape. I can see numerous gunshot wounds to both his legs. Thanh has pulled Wolf's trousers down and there's another bullet hole in the soft flesh just below his buttocks. He is lying in a growing pool of blood.

We need to get to Marauder as quickly as possible, but Wolf needs urgent treatment, he's haemorrhaging badly and any delay in getting him out could cost him his life. In an agony of uncertainty I glance about me at the reaction force—anxious eyes probing mine as I hesitate. There's a bomb hole further back, which we had passed on our way to this warren of bunkers. If we retrace our steps and secure the spot we could probably evacuate Wolf by helicopter, if the dustoff can get to us . . . *And what about Newman and the patrol?*

'I'll get Wolf out,' I say to Sonny. 'You press on. I'll keep Thanh, Pak and four Bodes with me.'

20 DUST-OFF FOR WOLF

The chopper gives that *crack crack crack* sound as the pilot pulls pitch in an attempt to break gravity's grip. The sound is identical to incoming rounds and I cast a wary glance at the jungle some 40 feet away from the bomb hole we're using as an LZ. The skids hover over my head as the dustoff pulls away, flailing the treetops with its propeller's wash. It's had two attempts at getting in, the first being aborted when heavy ground fire thwarted the approach, but finally Wolf is away and I'm relieved. He was semi-conscious when Thanh and I bundled him into the dustoff and the pallor of his skin left me concerned about his chances. Thanh had put an IV in, but it was of dubious value. Still, he'll be in Cu Chi within 40 minutes and lying on a gurney headed for the emergency surgical ward. I wonder what the surgeon will think when he sees the still healing gunshot wound. Ten minutes earlier the gripes had got to me again and I had been forced to seek privacy to relieve myself. I was in an untenable situation. On the one hand I needed space to preserve my dignity when my bowels let go; on the other, I required the security of the rest of the group in a very dangerous situation. I compromised by crapping on the edge of the bomb hole with one hand on the radio handpiece and the other on the pistol grip of my rifle.

Got to move. There are only six of us and Charlie knows where we are. I can hear the sound of small arms coming from the river, buoyed by the rattle of M-60 fire. I'm assuming that Sonny, Ruiz and the bulk of the Bodes have reached Bernie Newman. Jesus, I hope so . . .

We're moving now, backtracking towards the river in single file, two Bodes up front as scouts, me and Pak, Thanh and then tail-end charlie with an M-60. I'm concerned about Clyde chasing us up from the rear; we'd spent too much time at the LZ and I can hear noises, so I'm 'back heavy'. As we move through the forest the place looks familiar. We've reached the spider holes where Wolf was hit: scattered items of equipment confirm that. As I cast about me I see two empty M-16 magazines taped together on the trampled ground. Brass casings litter the area. A bandolier festoons a nearby bush, its tapes hanging like thick spaghetti in the leaves. We're closer to the river this time, so I can't see Jack-in-the box's hole, but I've no doubt he's still there, even though I'm sure he'll never perform another encore.

We press on through the tangle of bush, avoiding bamboo thickets that jut from the river. It's heavy going. Smoke drifts like haze amongst the tree trunks and I can smell burnt cordite. We're on a gentle slope and through a break in the canopy I catch glimpses of the river, it's just below us. The well-trodden path we're following divides at this point, with the left-hand fork paralleling the river. The right drops away to the bank. Our forward scout has reached the fork and . . . transfixed, I glimpse an enemy party jogging up the slope. I spot at least a dozen soldiers dressed in khaki uniforms and black pyjamas. The lead elements are carrying AK-47s. Close to the rear of the group is a pith-helmeted soldier trundling what looks like a wheeled heavy machine-gun. Behind him is a pyjama-clad VC with an RPG over his shoulder. Our forward scout opens fire at point-blank range and then drops out of sight. There's a sharp exchange of fire and number two scout comes rushing towards me, wide-eyed. 'Ayaaa . . .', he exclaims. His equipment, snagged by the foliage, is awry. He looks like a Christmas tree that's gone through a wind tunnel. 'Dai hui, dai hui beaucoup VC . . .' He risks a backward glance as he draws level with me. 'Di di mao!' he adds in a breathless voice and promptly pops his Buddha. I grab the man by the back of his harness and swing him around, surprised at how light he feels. There's no point in running back to where we came from, besides we're close to the rest of the reaction force and there's safety in numbers. I manhandle the Bode to the ground just as all hell breaks loose.

I can't hear myself think. A roaring storm overwhelms me. I'm vaguely aware of cracking noises and out of the corner of my eye I watch with bizarre fascination as bits of bark fly from the tree trunks just above me. Broken branches and clusters of leaves fall like rain. *Ptong . . . ptong . . .* I'm vaguely aware of Pak firing two M-79 grenade rounds, and then comes the sound of their detonation close to the junction in the track: *cranng . . . cranng . . .*

Superimposed on the snarl of M-16 fire comes the welcome yammering of the M-60 and I could jump for joy. Tail-end-charlie has always been my concern. I had watched him casting wistful glances in the direction of the LZ earlier on. It was plain he thought this was madness and if he had his druthers he'd rather be out there hitching a ride back on one of the slicks, getting the hell out of the place. So it gives me a warm feeling to know that the M-60 is still in the equation.

Boom, boom, boom . . . I can feel the recoil of the SLR against my shoulder—can't recall aiming the rifle let alone pulling the trigger. I'm baffled by the way the enemy seems hell-bent on wanting to reinforce this side of the river. I guess that the patrol we've just bumped into is attempting to outflank our reaction force and we've surprised them . . . and that the enemy has waited for a pause in our bombing to cross the river from Cambodia.

The sound of firing lifts in intensity as more and more of the enemy patrol fan out on this side of the river.

Craang . . .

An RPG has just gone off in the jungle not far from Pak and I crane my neck to see if he's alright. Lumps of dirt plop around us, and bits of tree branches crash through the foliage. Pak's okay and I wave to him to move closer. He slithers across like a snake and I reach for the handset of the radio. 'Marauder this is two nine alpha, you copy? Over.' It's hard to hear above all the booming and banging that's going on, so I repeat the call.

The radio is silent, not even the hiss of static when I free the squelch. And then I see it. A piece of shrapnel about the shape of a thumbtack has torn a path across the back of the radio's casing. The ANPRC-25 is as dead as a doornail!

I can hear movement to the right. The bastards are trying to flank us. The trouble is we're one skinny line, and once they get round that M-60 they've got us from the back. I cut a glance at the gunner who's crouching over his rucksack, scrabbling frantically to extract a spare belt of linked ammunition. His gun rests on its bipod, barrel smoking.

I'm of a mind to fall back and cover the rear, but if I do that it might send the wrong message to the Bodes. What if they take that as a signal to bug out? 'I go rear security,' Pak pre-empts me. He's obviously come to the same conclusion and I nod my head thankfully as he shucks off the useless radio. While he crawls away I cast a glance at the second scout. He hasn't moved since I dropped him. The man looks to be in shock, his eyes swivelling between Pak and me.

'You okay?' I ask. No answer. Perhaps he's weighing up his chances should he bolt. We're down to five weapons and I can't afford to lose one, but he's no good to me in a foetal position! 'No di di mao, huh,' I growl and he shakes his head—oh no, wouldn't think of it.

Out of the corner of my eye I see that the gunner has finished clipping his spare ammo to the belt. He ducks his head reflexively as green tracer fans in an arc over the river bend and towards the gunships circling Marauder. But our immediate concern is closer to hand and I'm glad to see the gunner's got his priorities sorted. He swings his M-60 to the right, letting go a five-round burst. I too fire a few rounds at fleeting shadows . . . got to watch the ammo. Shrugging my rucksack off my back I fish through my gear until I find three full magazines. I lay them out in front of me.

Underlying the sounds of battle is another sound. It's difficult to pick up at first, but nevertheless there. It is a sound that of itself is quite innocent, a sound that reminds me of distant suburban playing fields. But in this context, on the Cambodian border, it invokes terror. It is the eerie sound of whistle blasts.

21   SURVIVING A DANCE WITH THE BEAR

The body of the forward scout lies where it has fallen. From where I crouch, peering at it through the cover of the foliage, I know he's dead. He had fallen forward and his face is half buried in the debris, one eye staring back at me with a vague look of disinterest. I can't recognise this man, yet only a few minutes ago he was a living, working member of our reaction force. It's bizarre the way death changes the look of people. He's like a rag doll, arms hidden under his body, neck stretched out at an uncomfortable angle and face half buried.

While checking the posts of my little perimeter, a thought had flashed through my mind. *This is not a good place to make a bower.* Robbie's words—whatever made me think of them?

Major Bruce Robertson had been the 'major training' at Kapooka, the recruit training centre where I was posted on graduation. Robbie had been my mentor. He was typical of the World War II veteran officers the army had hung on to in order to bolster the inexperienced ranks. Robbie believed in hard work but had a cynical, almost iconoclastic, approach to the trappings of soldiering. The subalterns loved him. He was young at heart even though he must have been in his late forties. He always enjoyed the subalterns' stories of their latest conquests. There was a field hospital attached to the base and the nurses, members of the Australian Army Nursing Corps, were fair, if prohibited, game. We would have our nightly illicit trysts with the female NCOs from the hospital on Mount Pomingalarna, a bare hilltop in the training area, and then brag about these to Robbie. An eccentric when it came to romance, Robbie, whose fiancée at the time was the matron of the hospital, would often go for picnics. His penchant was to prepare what he called a 'bower', in which he would romance his fiancée after supping on champagne and chicken sandwiches prepared by the officers' mess kitchen. The bower was always a hollow in the ground that he would layer with aromatic wattle or lemon-scented tea-tree branches. He maintained that a good bower was one that provided adequate observation so that the subalterns could not catch him in the act.

There was an event of some excitement amongst the subalterns just before I left for my posting to New Guinea. That event was the arrival of the padre's daughter. She had been at boarding school and on graduation had returned to Kapooka. I had met her two years previously when she occasionally visited the officers' mess. She was a child then. Now, at sixteen she had lost the boyish lines of childhood. Her coltish legs had shaped nicely and flared hips had replaced jutting bones. Teddy Love, a fellow subaltern, and I were instantly in love. I don't think the girl was in love with us, but I *do* think she was infatuated by the fact that we, as 'older' men, were wooing her. In retrospect it was childish and quite immoral, but testosterone being what it is, you know . . . Anyway, Robbie confronted me in the mess one evening and gave me some words of advice regarding the dangerous ground I was treading. 'This is not a good place to make a bower,' he had said with a smile that could cut ice. I knew exactly what he meant.

This is not a good place to make a bower. The thought fell on me like the first swollen raindrop preceding a tropical deluge. I was leopard-crawling towards Pak's position, fatigued and uncertain, when I had this . . . this synaptic experience. But it didn't take long for my mind to clear itself of all those warm fuzzy characters from the past. We were about to be counterattacked, I sensed that, and Charlie would no doubt have registered the track junction as a target. After all, we were right in the guts of it. Pak had set out two claymores in a fan covering an arc of about 60 degrees. He glanced at me from behind a moss-covered buttress, wild-eyed and apprehensive, no doubt wondering what else I had in store for him, the claymore clackers resting beside his weapon. 'Blow them,' I rasped. 'We're getting the hell out of here.' Pak cocked his brow at me, uncertain of my intent, but when I mimed the action by hitting the palm of one hand with the other he got the message. The explosion sent a plume of brown smoke filtering through the bush and there were no more rustling sounds.

I retraced my steps to where I'd left the second scout, Pak following me, anxiously sweeping the rear as we moved. The second scout hadn't moved and there was no way I could trust him to take point. That left me with a choice between Pak, the gunner and Thanh the medic. To expose the M-60 at point would be imprudent, and Thanh could be sorely needed if we ran into more trouble. That left Pak. We exchanged glances and I could see he didn't want to go on, but I knew he would if I directed him to. His eyes had an unmistakable fatigue to them. He could probably do the job, but . . . I made a decision. I would lead. I motioned for the gunner to fall in behind me, gesturing for Pak to take the role of tail-end-charlie. And so we'd set off, gingerly stepping forward in the direction of the track junction. My heart was in my mouth as we moved without incident to the point where I'd found the forward scout.

Moving, moving past the forward scout—the rag doll with

the vacant staring eye—following the track that roughly parallels the river. Will we be able to come back to reclaim the body? We'll have to make every effort, but right now I'm too fatigued to care. The juices of energy have drained from me. I have an overwhelming desire to rest, to curl up in the jungle and go to sleep. It's a strange sensation. My eyelids are heavy and yet my heart hammers away, squirting adrenalin through a system that begs to be shut down.

A gentle rain starts to fall. It's quiet, except for the pattering of raindrops on leaves and the subdued metallic click of the gunner's ammo belt as it bumps against a harness buckle. It's irritating, but I'm too weary to stop the patrol and fix the problem. I know I should, but . . . I'm too tired. I wish I wasn't here—I wish . . . I wish I was *anywhere* but here. Even . . . even the Whang Pu rather than the Vam Co Dong . . . As a boy I hated the smell of the Whang Pu River. The pervasive smell of diesel oil on the Shanghai docks could not completely overcome the smell of mud and rotting vegetation that hung over the river. Once I saw a dead baby float by in the murky water.

My thoughts are drifting . . .

On Saturday nights, when I was in my teens, I'd inevitably find myself either at Cloudland in the Valley or the Blind Institute Hall in South Brisbane. It's not that I loved to dance so much, it's that the sheilas gathered there. My mates Paul George and Wally Nogin and I would gravitate there to chase sheilas. Sometimes we'd go to the O'Connor Boat House dance by the river, but that was never as good as Cloudland or the Institute, besides which the Boat House always conjured up visions of blistered hands and a sore bum; I rowed for the Commercial Rowing Club and it had its boats beneath the dance floor. We used to take off for our training sessions from the pontoon in front of the Boathouse.

The atmosphere of Cloudland was the thing. The blokes

would find themselves along the wall, waiting eagerly for the sheilas to arrive while the band tuned up their instruments. The best place to be was opposite the main entrance so that you were the first to view the sheilas as they wandered in—to make your pick, so to speak—and we'd often fight to get the best chairs along the wall. Oh yes, I remember getting my fair share of the best seats on the track.

Best seats on the *track?*

Sure. There were people there already and I'd have to hurry.

Best seats on the . . . TRACK?

The rain has petered out but heavy mist hangs in the trees. The track rounds a bend and I've stopped there, my mind trying to correlate the evidence of my eyes. There are blurred images of people squatting on the track! I'm frozen to the spot, the rabbit in my ribcage doing that inverted thing again. I can't believe I've allowed my concentration to lapse. It's Charlie on the track! I can see people dressed in khaki uniforms and black pyjamas silently squatting on the track—a row of Ho Chi Minh sandals! I can see the shapes of AK-47s and the VC closest to me has a Chinese stick grenade hanging off his belt. He wears a pith helmet and there's rain dripping off its brim into his lap. And then it comes to me in a flash. This is a counterattack force. The VC we'd bumped earlier on were probably reinforcements coming from across the river to join it, and I'm standing at the edge of their assembly area! Jesus Christ . . .

I'm so preoccupied with my revelations that I've almost missed the arrival of the gunner. He too has blundered onto the track. Pith helmet looks up at exactly the moment the gunner registers the presence of the VC and that tableau, frozen in time, will be with me for the rest of my life. Suddenly the M-60 comes to life. The gun's muzzle flash sears the skin of my forearm as red tracer dances down the track. The gunner moves forward in little rushes, firing from the hip. The M-60's a big weapon and the gunner's struggling to control it—tracer stitching upwards into the treetops. The shiny brass belt of bullets jerks and writhes at each burst as it feeds into the maw of the M-60's breech. The man's about to run out of ammo! And he's still upright, leaning back to balance the weight of the smoking gun. I crawl forward along the track and just as the gunner runs out of ammunition, I fire a burst from my SLR. It sounds just like the M-60. 'Get down,' I scream and the gunner drops, looking as though he has suddenly awakened from a dream.

Booom . . . booom.

The shots reverberate through my skull . . . smashing glass . . . flares sprout like blossoms against a darkening sky . . .

The ground is shaking . . . explosions . . . there's firing . . . star-shaped flashes festoon the undergrowth like cheap, sparkling trinkets . . . fireflies in the night. There's a roar . . . oh so loud. And then a sonic boom and a dreadful all-pervading smell of gasoline fumes that hang like a pall over everything. There's a pause that seems to stretch into forever and then more roaring as the second fighter swoops. *Enough.* I cut a glance at the gunner. His shoulders convulse as he retches. *Enough! Enough!*

'ENOUGH!' I scream, but no one hears. In the midst of this cacophony there are no sane ears to hear . . . there is no sane will, there's only madness.

And then there's liquid fire. A rolling plume of oily fire that roars and hisses and consumes, a fire that towers over 200-year-old buttresses and makes them disappear. I feel a sucking wind like a tornado that draws everything towards its maw. I can't breathe! And the heat's so intense that it makes your exposed skin blister. *Enough . . .*

Oh dear God please let there be peace . . .

Peace . . .
Frè-re Jacques, Frè-re Jacques . . .

The huge wrought iron gates of St Jean D'Arc College open inwards. The clean-swept stone pavers lead to a broad expanse of driveway with aspens bordering either side. Pop used to say that the sight of the aspens always made him nostalgic for Mother Russia. My spirits are uplifted as I skip through the gates. I can see Grandpop's car down the drive, waiting to pick me up.

Dor-mez vous, dor-mez vous . . .

As a day pupil I can escape in the early afternoon, and it's only the ditty—voices in child-like harmony—emanating from a junior class window that still links me with the place.

Son-nez les matines, son-nez les matines . . .

The song resounds within the walls of the college, piping young voices within the sombre walls of the main building. Walls with rising damp, overgrown by ivy . . .

I despised the Brothers at the College. They were brusque country bumpkins, too quick to punish even minor infringements, and I felt their piety before God was contrived. I remember the day the head Brother and two of his housemasters came to our place for dinner. Pop had invited them so I could meet them outside the school environment. It also gave my parents an opportunity to get to know them better. At first the conversation had been stilted, but Pop fed them a few drinks and in next to no time they were chattering like monkeys. The Brothers wore black cassocks with a detachable white plastic bib on their collars and my mother, in particular, warmed to one of the big raw-boned housemasters. When she asked him whether he kept his sermon notes on the back of his bib, he replied, 'No. Just girlfriends' telephone numbers.' That one brought the house down! But they scared the hell out of me, and more than one of them had left the imprint of his hand on my bottom. Still, I guess I was no angel . . .

Fire flares and crackles in the jungle. Shadows dance across the track. There are two pyjama-clad bodies lying on the track and . . . and the gunner's down. I see his face twisted in pain, a spreading blossom of blood saturating the front of his shirt. Thanh is crouched beside him. Pak is on the other side of me, wedged against the flanged root of a tree. 'Dai hui, napalm,' Pak says, jerking his chin in the direction of the fireball. His grin is wide enough to swallow a watermelon. As I lie hugging the damp ground with the sound of fire in my ears and the smell of gasoline redolent in my nostrils, my hands shake uncontrollably.

In the midst of this confusion I can hear the unmistakable sound of an approaching Bird Dog. There's a hole in the canopy above the track and through it I can see the silvery shape of the Cessna as it zooms low over the trees. It's Smokey Barnes! He's down at treetop level, doing damage assessment I guess, and my spirits are instantly uplifted at the improbable sight of the jolly little plane in the middle of this carnage. *Those magnificent men in their fly-ying machines, they go uppity up up, they go dowwnn down down . . .* With the silly words of the song ringing in my head, a nervous irrational fit of the giggles infects me, much to the consternation of Pak, who looks at me as if I've taken leave of my senses. And then the seriousness of the situation hits me. Most likely Barnes saw Pak, Thanh or myself on the track. He *probably* would have spotted the bodies. He would have tried the radio if he had any doubts as to who we were . . .

And then I hear that buzzing sound again—the Bird Dog returning! Only this time I'm gripped by the dreadful possibility that Barnes has mistaken us for VC and is at this moment marshalling Christ knows what air resources to dump on us! The buzz saw is getting louder all the time and I dread the arrival of that silvery hull as it fills the patch of sky above the canopy. Pak has obviously gone through the same deductive process, but he is one step ahead of me. He snatches the red, white and blue kerchief from around his neck, and just as the Cessna appears he points the bandanna skywards, holding it in both hands and snapping it a number of times like a marker panel. The plane disappears out of sight and I'm left with its receding sound and the blood drumming in my temples. I crouch in the mud, a riot of doubts and conflicting questions crowding my mind.

But there's another sound on the left flank, an unmistakable noise of people moving through the jungle, snapping twigs and stepping on deadfall. I gesture for Pak to take cover. He waves at me. 'Is alright,' he whispers, beaming. 'Task For.' And he's right. Out of the fog of smoke comes a long line of tiger suits.

I recognise Pridemore, and there's Wiskow! It's two nine bravo . . . the rest of my reaction force! I can see Bodes crashing around in the jungle everywhere. Some of them have made up bush poles threaded through ponchos in which lie the wounded, others are dragging wounded along the ground in makeshift slings made up of ponchos and ground sheets. There must be at least 30 in the group. Behind the stretcher-bearers comes the party of walking wounded, shambling along as quickly as they can. Suddenly the place is full of troops, friendly troops, and there's the sound of approaching helicopters.

I can't remember how I got to the LZ but here I am. I pile aboard the chopper crowded with people, weapons and gear, the *ginnie ginnie wop wop* sound of its rotors ringing oh so sweetly in my ears and the wind blasting in all directions. I'm vaguely aware of the fact that Newman and I are the last to leave the LZ; it's an eerie feeling to look at that deserted open field knowing that there are no friendlies back there.

Bernie Newman is beside me now. From a crumpled pack he fishes out two bent cigarettes and lighting them with a Zippo, he hands me one. There's a tired old smile on his face as he contentedly blows a stream of smoke through his nostrils which is quickly whipped away by the buffeting wind. I lean back against the metal stanchion beside the door gunner's cradle, my feet dangling over the skids, trouser legs flapping like pennants in a gale. I close my eyes and breathe a long sigh of relief, only now assimilating the fact that Bernie and I have indeed survived this dance with the bear.

22

JANIS AND JOHN MAKE WAY FOR GRITZ'S SONG

The command and control detachment at the end of the airstrip at Tay Ninh, B-32, is a fortified camp with a circular outer berm surrounded by a barbed-wire entanglement. Its task is to provide support to the Special Forces border surveillance camps in War Zone C. A company of indigenous troops has fighting positions dug into the berm as well as sleeping bays, and many of the soldiers have brought their wives and children into the camp. These families, together with their dogs and chickens, live with the soldiers in the outer berm. The command tolerates this, probably reasoning that the presence of his family adds incentive for a soldier to fight that much harder in the event of an attack. And attacked they were one night, when the Task Force drove a truck through the Bamboo Bar. However, no indigenous soldier attempted to repel the marauders that night and it was a measure of Sergeant Major Bowen's tolerance that nothing further had come of the incident. Bowen had served with the MGF before it had become the Task Force and he knew the pressure the men were under. The Task Force paid for the damages and the air-conditioned bar at B-32 continued to be the pressure safety valve.

This night the Bamboo Bar is unusually quiet. Normally the penetrating voice of Janis Joplin assails the eardrums of anyone within 100 yards. As a rule Ms Joplin gives forth with a raunchy rendition of 'Bye Bye Baby' or some other momentous song. If not Joplin, then John Denver's nostalgic tones fill the air from the speakers of the Akai tape recorder above the line of back-lit bottles. But the night the Task Force returned from the Vam Co Dong River there was no music. In deference, the barman had kept Janis and John muzzled, the black leather button-down stools being occupied by silent and sombre people.

I study the bar, noting the missing faces. Martin's not here, neither are Aleo, Deo or Bradley. Wolf is missing, so too are Burr and Grant. There are others as well, Stark is one of them. I guess they're all at Cu Chi or 36 Evac Hospital in Vung Tau. Some of them would be lying on gurneys. But for Simmons, Taylor and Tabouda there's a different resting place . . . I'm on my fourth Mister Daniel, hence my maudlin state, and Newman is beside me.

He's talking to someone at the bar about his predicament just before the reaction force arrived. 'Martin had the radio on the tactical frequency and he gets a call from someone wanting to know if we could use some gunships,' says Newman. 'I tell Martin to ask him if he's got any ground troops. Martin comes back, No, but he wants to send in some gunships.' Newman shakes his head. 'I got all the air I need so I told Martin to tell this guy to fuck off the net. Martin follows orders for once in his life. He says, "My oh six marauder told me to tell you to fuck off the net, over." Just before Martin takes his ride in the medivack, I ask him who the hell was that on the net? Martin says, "I don't know but his call sign was Tropic Lightning something." Newman gives that yuk-yuk chuckle of his and says, 'Martin had just told the deputy divisional commander of the 25th Infantry Division to fuck off.'

I've never been one for drinking hard liquor, preferring beer, but lately I've been seduced by the heady power of bourbon. I glance at Newman. Even after half an hour in a steaming tub there's still a vague odour of shit emanating from him—the price one pays for spending time in a VC crapper. Sonny has given up and moved to another section of the bar. He is truly the essence of tolerance! There's not much conversation going on. Newman and I are slugging drinks and I'm staring vacantly at the rings of condensation from our glasses accumulating on the table. I see Mister Daniel as a sea of amber with an iceberg floating in it. It's an endless sea from which there is no escape for me. My dance with the bear has turned out alright, but it was line-ball. What about next time? I don't know how many more of these I can survive. I don't dare to think about home and I ache too much whenever I think of my wife. Just to touch her smooth skin and feel her silky clothes ... just to smell the scent of her ... But not here, not at the Bamboo Bar with its back-lit bottles and sombre faces and haunted eyes bespeaking a horror in which the tatters of madness are never far from the surface.

In a hesitant voice someone starts up a song that's vaguely familiar:

Shall we gather at the river ...

The voice is not particularly melodious, but there's something about the old Salvation Army tune that's riveting. And besides, the choirboy is gathering confidence:

Yes, we'll gather at the river,
The beautiful, the beautiful river ...

And then another choirboy joins in with his own variation:

If you shot 'em in the water,
Major Gritz'll give you another quarter ...

Right on cue the Task Force choristers give voice now,

booming dulcet tones ricocheting off the walls of the smoke-filled bar, filling the place with a strange nostalgia.

Yes we'll gather at the river
Major Gritz's blessed river
The beautiful, the beautiful river
Gather with the saints of the river . . .

I can feel the lump in my throat growing and my hands have started to shake again. The iceberg rattles perilously in its sea of amber.

23

27 January '68.

Whirling dervishes of dust twisted on the blacktop as the late afternoon sun cooked the airstrip at the FOB. The radio in the commo tent made desultory crackling sounds, stirring the duty signalman from his torpor. The man cast a sleepy eye in my direction and waved to me. I picked up the headset. It was Wildcat. He wanted volunteers for a special mission. The requirement was to get the volunteers to Bien Hoa as quickly as possible. I glanced about me. The Hulk, stripped to his tiger suit pants and jungle boots, was giving some hapless LRRP an 'ear reaming'—holding the LRRP's head steady while inserting his tongue into the man's ear amidst raucous laughter. Hulk was one of the walking wounded and was supposed to be in hospital, but who the hell could hold him there? Bernie Newman and John Aiello were egging him on. Sonny Edwards sat like a little chubby Buddha, his bare shoulders lily white in contrast to his florid face. He seemed as though he were meditating. Perhaps he was preparing himself for the movie *Brazos* (or something like that) that Beatty had got for us. With a name like that I expected it to be full of Mexican fury and dark-eyed ladies of the night, so I guess it was worth meditating over. Jerry Burr was in deep conversation with the Saint, who sat in a corner with a beatific grin on his face. Maybe he thought he was stalking Ho Chi Minh himself. Needless to say, we had all been drinking. I didn't dwell too long on the problem of selection. 'You're all bloody volunteers! We're off to Bien Hoa. Get dressed,' I bellowed above the din. Talk about a snowball effect. By the time I got to the tarmac our numbers had grown. Not only did we have the Task Force, but the gunships were also warming up for take-off. 'Are we ready?' I asked Bernie.

'Armed and dangerous,' Newman replied as we clambered aboard the choppers. All I could see was a motley lot of greens and tiger suits with red, white and blue scarves disappearing into the helicopters. I can just imagine the effect it must have had as our little armada of five slicks and a light-fire team dropped into Bien Hoa like hornets into a paddock of gently grazing cattle.

We landed on the Bien Hoa soccer field with the gunships doing a dry run around the slicks as we disembarked—a sort of honour roll. Gritz and Critchley met us. They had two trucks parked on the edge of the field. 'Here we are, ready to go, Sir,' I boomed over the noise of the choppers.

'My God, Kraz, did you have to bring the entire unit?' Gritz chuckled.

'Sir? You said all volunteers for an especially tough mission. Well, here we are.'

I thought I must be in a cage full of baboons, judging by the babble and raucous laughter behind me.

'Secure all your weapons and gear, shut down the birds and assemble everyone for pick-up. Critch, load 'em up. Get 'em to the club. Unarmed.'

Crighton stood to attention and gave an exaggerated wind-up British salute. 'Sah!' he bellowed.

We were all deposited at the front of the enlisted men's club and ushered inside, 50 or so of us, counting aircrew. There were long Formica-topped tables in the centre of the room with jars of peanuts and the like spread around and we commandeered two of these. As if by magic five bottles of Mister Daniel and another five of Mister Beam appeared. The peanuts and crisps were tipped out of their containers and replaced by a witch's brew of Mister Daniel and Mister Beam. Filled to the brim, the containers were passed around the table so that each of us could sup in turn. This strange behaviour had not passed unnoticed and a distinct space was being maintained between the Task Force and the remaining patrons of the club. A visiting strip show from Australia was the feature entertainment planned for the evening.

The show started reasonably well with long-legged strippers in flimsy pearl-sequinned outfits performing against some racy background music, but things deteriorated rapidly. It was too much for the unshaven rowdies of the Task Force, some of whom immediately propositioned the performers. Under different circumstances I'm sure arrangements could have been made, but the sight of these bearded strange-looking people must have been extremely off-putting to the girls, who were used to being pampered.

The music and the dancers faltered. Disgusted by the less than enthusiastic response from the ladies and bored by a lacklustre performance, someone shot out the lights at one end of the stage with a silenced pistol. I cast a glance at Gritz, registering the fact that he too had noticed what had happened. We were headed for trouble unless he did something, and fast. 'Follow me, men,' Gritz snapped, jumping to his feet. With that he led us all single file out of the club and into the fresh air and I breathed a sigh of relief, but my optimism was short lived. We were like a super-critical mass ready to explode and in search of touch-paper.

The pinnacle of US military diplomacy in the area was the III Corps Vietnamese Officers' Club. In Vietnamese it was called the Cau Lac Bo and that's where we were headed for, travelling the well-laid paths of the base. It was Saturday evening and the base was crowded with off-duty staff immaculately dressed in green fatigues and spit-shined boots, but as we wobbled along, the Indian file looking more like a dog's hind leg, the path in front of us was rapidly clearing.

I have the bizarre recollection that on our way to the Cau Lac Bo we detoured via the morgue, but for the life of me I could never swear that that was so. Perhaps it's a figment of my imagination, born of the nightmares I subsequently experienced, or perhaps I was simply very drunk at the time and my mind was playing tricks. I don't know, but I have the impression of marching past long sliding metal drawers in the cold room within which bodies were laid out. Every time Gritz saw one of our men in those drawers he would stand raptly at attention and salute. There were quite a few salutes given, but as I say, I don't really know. Maybe by that time Mister Beam and Mister Daniel were truly fucking with my head.

As fate would have it, the Cau Lac Bo on that Saturday evening was entertaining Premier Ky and many high-ranking Vietnamese military dignitaries were present. Various US garrison chiefs were also represented. There was a string orchestra playing and the club was decked out in streamers and party balloons. The place was also crawling with Quan Canh, the Vietnamese Security Police. The QCs as they were called wore white helmet liners and carried chrome snub-nosed .38 revolvers in white blancoed holsters strapped to equally snow-white web belts. They wore dark sunglasses even after sunset and well-fitting starched green uniforms and behaved like martinets with the airs and graces of a privileged class. And, because of the authority vested in them and their arrogance, they were extremely dangerous.

Premier Ky had just departed by the front door as we arrived by the back. Gritz's usual entrance was through the kitchen door and we made our way, still in Indian file, past a table with steaming noodles, chicken legs and Christ knows what else. The floor was littered with fly-spotted chicken entrails and fish heads: though the place looked like shit, the smell was surprisingly appetising. As we entered the grand ballroom where couples were dancing, the music wavered momentarily and the head violinist stared at us, aghast. I could almost hear the collective intake of breath as the luminaries present digested our sudden appearance. In the meantime, oblivious to it all, Gritz had his arm around the club mama-san's ample waist and was busily arranging things.

It was a measure of the respect the staff had for Bo Gritz that we were ushered to a prominent section of the ballroom and a row of tables was set for us. The musicians picked up again, at first with some trepidation but then, heartened by the fact that their worst fears had not been realised, they struck up with gusto. However, I noticed that the manager was still sceptical, casting suspicious glances at the assembled Task Force whose appearance was most likely reminiscent of a group of escapees from a lunatic asylum. He approached a group of several QCs and had a whispered conversation with them.

Oblivious to the undercurrent of tension that hovered over the ballroom, some of the boys had popped a few bottles of champagne and were making merry. Gritz sought to reassure the QCs that all would be well, that the Task Force was just here for an overnight R&R and that we'd all be gone after a few drinks to celebrate the occasion of Premier Ky's visit. What bullshit, I thought, but it was a side of Bo that I had not seen before. It was obvious that he could be extremely diplomatic when he chose to.

The trouble started when some of the boys, unimpressed by the genteel music, took to singing in opposition. I must say the minstrels were off key and out of tune, but they looked happy. I noticed one of the QCs moving in on Bernie Newman. *Oh-oh, bad move*, I thought. Here was this martinet about to play hardball and of all people Newman was a poor choice to do so with. As the QC reached forward to manhandle Newman, Aiello 'pacified' him by rapping him on his helmet liner with the barrel of his .45 automatic. To lend emphasis to the fact that it was *not* a good idea to fuck with the Task Force, Aiello then fired two shots into the ceiling.

Well, the next few minutes provided a psychological insight into humanity. To the accompaniment of shattering window glass and shrieking female voices, well-dressed men in suits unceremoniously pushed slender women in ao dais out of the way to get under tables. Staff officers and civilians bumped into each other as they rushed about in panic, searching for a safe exit. At one stage I remember seeing Gritz standing on a chair yelling 'tay oh,' but then my mind had been worked over by Mister Beam and Mister Daniel and may well have left me in a state of hallucination. As if by magic the QCs had disappeared, having beaten a hasty retreat when Aiello's starting gun had gone off.

And then there was quiet. Through the fog of plaster dust I could see members of the Task Force taking up strategic positions around the devastated ballroom. I was wondering what the next step would be. Prudently Crighton had locked up most of our weapons on arrival so I knew we couldn't sustain an extended siege. In the distance I could hear the *wop wop* of helicopters.

'Reinforcements,' Sonny growled, peeking from around the shattered front door of the Cau Lac Bo. 'Bet that's the MP Company from Saigon.' He craned his neck to get a better look outside. 'Coming to take over from the local dickheads.' A drunken smile was plastered to his face.

I cast about me, scanning the wreckage. Tattered multicoloured streamers trailed from the corners of the ballroom. Two or three balloons had survived the shootout. Upturned tables littered the floor and the place had a sparkling layer of broken glass. We camped in this ravaged landscape, a little stunned and glassy-eyed. The power had been turned off and long shadows spiked and crisscrossed the ballroom from a single spotlight out in the street somewhere, aimed at the building. I wondered if this was the kind of scene that prompted Salvador Dali to do his best work.

After what seemed to be an eternity but would have been no more than fifteen minutes, we heard a growing number of excited voices rising and falling, coming from the darkness of the street. And finally: 'Come out with your hands up.' The metallic voice, much magnified, came through a bullhorn.

'You want us, you come and get us.' The words coming from the back of the ballroom were barely audible even to me squatting just a few paces away. There was no threat in the tone of voice, just the inevitable tenor of a cornered gunfighter. I could sense the sentiment. We all felt the same way, a reflection of months of facing the enemy at close quarters with all the horror and uncertainty that carried. No one was coming out with his hands up, and when I realised that it occurred to me that I might die here. And even as the thought struck me, I felt a sense of outrage. We were the soldiers of the conqueror, the Task Force. Ours was to rape, loot and plunder. Just kidding. Actually I had just thrown up in the corner and felt like shit. And looking about me I realised that the others weren't much better off. The erstwhile minstrels now looked more like the despondent folk out of *Les Misérables,* but none of that assuaged my anger.

Time dragged on and nothing happened. From outside the occasional sound of voices continued, and the mournful wail of sirens. No one attempted to enter and break the standoff. And then it dawned on me that if we remained where we were,

SHADOWS ON THE WALL

the resolution would surely rest in the hands of the smooth-faced, guitar-strumming, ballad-singing staff pukes of Company A—intolerable. The thought must also have struck Gritz. He clambered to his feet, dusted himself off and said: 'Okay men, break up into small teams, let's get out of here.'

To the Task Force which was habitually used to breaking out under pressure, this was nothing new, but it unnerved the military police. As Gritz, Critchley and I started down the elevated stairs of the club, I witnessed a company of MPs frantically trying to withdraw in the face of fleeting shadows. One of their jeeps, the driver spooking, backed up so fast it ran over Sonny Edwards, who at the time was negotiating a back street in the company of the Hulk and two others.

As Gritz and I ran up to Sonny, I noticed the Hulk holding point, his .45 aimed at the jeep that was rapidly disappearing around a corner, still in reverse. Once Sonny got excited he was almost incoherent and I can tell you he was pretty pissed off at that moment, sitting in the road. He continued to pour out a torrent of unintelligible abuse as Gritz and the Hulk hefted him to his feet. As we walked briskly away, supporting Sonny who was still venting his spleen, Gritz turned to the Hulk and said, 'What the hell's he tryin' to say?'

'He says his damn leg is broke.'

'What?'

'Yessir. That's what I make of it. His leg's busted.'

'His leg can't be broken. Look how good he's been walking.'

Just before dawn Newman woke me. I had slept the sleep of the dead on the lawn in front of the Company A headquarters building, my head resting against one of the white-painted landscape boulders that lined the paths. As I painfully rubbed the crick in my neck I observed other bodies scattered over the lawn like sleeping cattle. 'You seen the major? Colonel Hayes is after him,' Newman growled. We did a swift body count but failed to find Gritz. 'I think I know where he is,' said

Newman and we both headed for Cambode Alley, just beyond the base perimeter. Sure enough, Gritz was in the house he rented for his girlfriend and Newman and I woke him up. 'Sir, you better get dressed. Colonel Hayes wants to see you an hour ago.' We waited while Gritz got dressed. His green fatigue jacket had bloodstains in the front. Gritz cocked a quizzical eyebrow. 'Must have been side-stream from one of the QCs.' Newman chuckled.

'Better round up the men, take them to the bar and keep them locked up until I'm finished with the colonel,' said Gritz. He was referring to the bar his mama-san ran in Cambode Alley.

Newman and I lined up the Task Force and we made our way down deserted streets to the bar to await our fate. Throughout the journey we were escorted by a platoon of military police backed up by a jeep with a .50 calibre machine-gun mounted in the back and pointed at us. I couldn't give a damn, my guts were rolling and I had a splitting headache.

Though I wasn't privy to the conversation between Gritz and the colonel, Bo did write about it in his book, *Called To Serve*. I believe the dialogue is worth noting:

'Bo, why do you do things like last night?'

'I don't know, Sir. It just seemed like the thing to do at the time.'

'Do you know that they think it was me that was in charge of that riot?'

'How's that sir? It was plainly B-36.'

'It's that damned bleached out major's leaf. It looked silver to the QCs. I had to personally apologize to the Commanding General of III Corps Tactical Zone this morning. For God's sake, Bo, the Provost Marshal from Saigon called our duty officer to advise him that they were sending a reinforced MP battalion after your guys ran the locals off.'

'What did the duty officer say?'

'He's new in Vietnam, but he'd heard about B-36 and he strongly suggested that the MP colonel save his troops.'

'What now, sir?'

'The Vietnamese Commanding General says you're no longer welcome in III Corps, the cities that is. You are to take your men and go back to the jungle. Bo, a final question: You have the best combat unit in Vietnam. Why can't you also have the best garrison unit?'

'I don't know, Sir. We just seem to be in a different army, fighting a war in a different world than yours. Sometimes we have to leave the real world.'

'Bo,' Colonel Hayes interrupted with an understanding tone to his voice, 'you're right.' With that he reached into his desk drawer and withdrew a double handful of human bones. His eyes took on a maniacal look as his voice raced to a fever pitch. 'You're right, Bo, this is the unreal world. Now go back where you belong.'

Meantime we sat at the bar like zombies, drinking iced water and looking at each other like naughty schoolchildren caught by the teacher. Actually the place was so rowdy you couldn't hear yourself think. During the course of the morning two ring-ins had found their way into the bar. They were strangers from some outfit in the Delta, otherwise they would have known about the Task Force. Anyhow, they tried to bum drinks off some of the boys, which was bad enough, but when they asked whether we belonged to the local ruff puff unit, it was too much. Both of them found themselves unconscious on the floor and equanimity was restored. In the midst of all this, with the drinks flowing freely, Gritz returned. He looked pale and somewhat shaken.

Newman sidled up to him. 'You know, Sir, no combat-ready unit ever passed an inspection and no inspection-ready unit ever passed combat,' he said with a broad grin. The bar smelt like a giant urinal. This was home.

Gritz looked about him. 'Where are the others?'

'This is it, Sir,' I said. 'The aircrews are standing by with the rest of the men to go wherever you say.'

'We're going back to the jungle. We shot our wad here in one night. The Commanding General's ordered us out of the cities.'

There was a low groan around the bar. 'Sir,' I implored, 'you promised us a weekend and this is only Saturday morning. Let's go somewhere else, we'll all be real good. Won't we, fellas?' I looked around at the bedraggled minstrels. Their faces had brightened at the prospect.

'Guys, I don't know anywhere far enough.'

'I do,' interjected one of the pilots who had remained behind. 'A great place with beaches, broads and booze.'

'How about it, Sir? We'll really be good.' The Hulk's angelic plea sounded so genuine.

'Okay. Saddle up, but at the first sign of trouble we're headed back to Tay Ninh.'

Five slicks, one C&C ship and a light-fire team took off from that soccer field in Bien Hoa with pieces of gaily coloured feminine apparel floating in the backwash, and I could imagine the collective sigh of relief that would have been breathed by the guitar-playing ballad singers of Company A upon our departure.

We circled Vung Tao like eagles in search of prey and plunder and it certainly looked like a place of booty. The hamlet nestling behind sand dunes looked like an inviting pearl. 'That's the Grand Hotel,' the Hulk roared above the din as the lead chopper banked to the left. 'See that white building? Put her down there.' He stabbed a finger in the direction of a building enclosed by a high stucco fence. Never mind aviation safety procedures. Just put this goddamned bird there. Oh boy.

In a cloud of dust, swirling sections of thatched roof and frantic chickens, the Task Force inserted into the walled garden of the Grand Hotel. We'd been in the place no more than three or four hours, imbued with the sensation of paradise, when in walked two MPs in search of Major Gritz. Apparently the commander of the Vung Tao airfield had placed our aviation unit under arrest for dangerous flying! Surrounded by a bevy of bar girls, Gritz and Critchley were holding court as the two MPs walked in. There was no one more prominent in the group of ladies than Kim Jane.

Kim Jane was a product of Vietnam's recent past, the result of the union of a French colonial woman and a mid-level Japanese administrator of the Imperial occupation force during World War II. I can only imagine how hard life would have been for a girl growing up in a country that despised the brutality of the Japanese during their occupation of Indochina. The subsequent war against the colonialist French would not have enamoured the other half of her family to the Vietnamese either. If life was hard in her first years, however, it was nothing by comparison to being orphaned, her parents having been killed by the Viet Minh in 1954. But Kim Jane had succeeded and the result was most pleasing to the eye. Taller than the Vietnamese, she was a voluptuous redhead, unusual for an Oriental woman to say the least, who was immediately besotted by the Task Force in general and its all-conquering leader in particular. In the end, so adamant was she that she wanted to 'sat cong—kill Viet Cong' that Gritz acquiesced and had her trained as a member of a hatchet team. It has been said that returning from a mission involving the destruction of a bridge in Cambodia she had yelled to her team leader, above the engine noise of the chopper that was extracting them, that she would prefer to go on the next operation wearing flip-flops on her feet as they would be more comfortable. In time Kim Jane too became a Task Force legend and could dress and carry whatever she pleased.

At the time, however, Kim Jane was a stripper at the Grand Hotel. 'No worries,' she said smiling. 'I know air force colonel. We fix.' Careful not to throw a damper on spirits, the senior of the two MPs said: 'Sir, you've got another problem.' He then told us that the Saint was being held by the local provost sergeant. Apparently he was in goal for assault with a deadly weapon and intent to commit murder. The MP's polite demeanour seemed out of character, but I assumed his cohorts in Saigon would have briefed him about the Cau Lac Bo incident the previous night and he certainly looked a bit spooked. I glanced at Gritz and then Newman, their eyes reflecting the same disbelief that I felt. Why would the Saint want to kill somebody for fun?

We went to see the air force colonel first, with Gritz leading, Newman, Kim Jane and yours truly in tow. Kim Jane was right. Her presence soothed the colonel's fevered brow. He looked embarrassed, casting glances at Kim Jane as he outlined his case: Vung Tao was a quiet hamlet used for R&R and not the place for 50 or so guerilla fighters.

Gritz straightened his diplomatic beret and launched into his spiel about the long mission the Task Force had just completed and the need his men had for some I&I rather than R&R. He defined I&I as 'intercourse and intoxication'. It was then that the colonel played his other card. Apparently not to be outdone, one of our aircrew had hung from the chopper strut throwing smoke grenades at people on the beach while the pilot flew the craft below treetop level. I tell you, this stuff is catching. At any rate, thanks to Kim Jane who by this time had pulled her chair right up beside the colonel, the matter was smoothed over with promises that the Task Force would remain caged within the bounds of the Grand Hotel and not be allowed to rape, plunder or in any other way bugger around the rest of the good folk of the hamlet.

Our next stop was to visit the provost marshal who informed us that the Saint was locked up in solitary confinement because of the serious nature of the charges laid against him. This was ominous. Gritz called the provost marshal aside, informing him in a hush-hush manner that the Task Force was a special operations unit that was about to depart on a critical mission. Sergeant First Class André Saint Laurent was a vital part of the unit and the provost marshal would be doing his country a real service if he released him from confinement so that he could be questioned further. They brought the Saint out. He looked like shit.

'Saint, what happened?' Gritz asked.

'Sir, you know how I don't like to mix with crowds and all, well I found this nice girl. She wanted to take me home. I bought some beer and we were going up the stairs to her place when this guy shows up and starts giving her a real hard time.'

'Oh he in love,' Kim Jane piped up, placing an understanding hand on the Saint's shoulder.

'So what did you do?'

'I asked him to quit, but he wouldn't. I just hit him over the head with my pistol. He got the cops and here we are.'

Gritz went into his act. Scowling at the Saint, he reminded him of the intended use of the 9 mm Browning and that if the Saint had used it properly, the guy wouldn't have been able to complain and none of this would have happened. The provost marshal was cutting glances at Gritz, partly suspicious of being the butt of a joke yet discomfited by the possibility that indeed he was in the presence of a bunch of homicidal maniacs. Kim Jane leaned over the Saint and gave him a peck on the cheek. 'Oh he in love,' she repeated as though that explained everything. It was a kiss of absolution and it unsettled the provost marshal even more. Taking advantage of the situation,

Gritz assured the provost marshal that he would personally punish the accused. With a show of reluctance that I believe harboured relief, the provost marshal signed the Saint over and we went back to the party. It's interesting to note that the Saint took Gritz's admonishment to heart. In 1970 he shot and killed a man in Vung Tao. He was found guilty by a court martial and sent to Leavenworth, only to have the judgment reversed on appeal. Saint Laurent was subsequently promoted to the rank of master sergeant.

While Aleo, aka the Wop, was in charge of stolen property and captured enemy equipment, Handwerk, who had more morals than a Trappist monk, was the Task Force bagman. Hand Job could be relied upon to be present at the critical moment to smooth over ruffled feathers, but because the Task Force in party mode moved rapidly and in all directions he gave up on the idea of paying for damages at the end. Mama-san would live in Handy's pocket throughout the night. So when Beatty, Hillman and I had a shooting contest from the veranda of the Grand Hotel, there were Handwerk and mama-san—the odd couple. Coloured lights festooned the walled garden below and the three of us were using these for targets. I had never been a good shot with a handgun and the dozen or so bottles of local Ba-muoi-ba beer I had drunk had not helped my accuracy. Suffice it to say that my two confrères were no better off. We hit very few lights, impacting all our rounds into the stucco wall. Even so, mama-san demanded payment for the loss of customers in the beer garden area. I failed to see why, seeing anyone who chose to could safely have sat in the garden. They might get a bit of cement dust in their drinks every now and then, but so long as they kept their heads down, no sweat. And what's a bit of cement dust in the rum and coke? Gritz, after all, was constantly having his drink stirred by the Hulk, and the Hulk was using the barrel of his .45 automatic to do it— Mister Daniel and rifle oil. Now *that* is an acquired taste. But

Bo Gritz was basically not a drinker, much preferring the company of the fair sex to carousing, and the bar girls were bedazzled by his charm.

He certainly had a way with women. I remember one time we were spending a night in Bien Hoa and he informed me that he was going to stay with his girlfriend in his rented house in Cambode Alley. 'I've gotta lower my sperm count,' he'd said with a grin. Which was fine except for two things. First, he wanted me to ride shotgun, and that meant breaching the night curfew and being out of bounds, and second, it meant spending a night in an area that was known to be used by the VC. We travelled the circuitous route to his house in pitch darkness through numerous alleyways heavy with the stench of human excreta, disturbing dogs and chickens and God knows what else on the way. I don't know how Gritz found his way, but he did with unerring accuracy and we were soon ensconced in the 'hau' as his girlfriend called it—a small two-roomed cement stuccoed building next to a market. It was plain that Bo was in his element and he showed no concern at the tenuous position we were in. He disappeared for the night while I mounted guard in the other room, ready to jump at every surreptitious noise. I'm convinced that he had a preconception of his destiny and a belief in his immortality. I wish I shared his beliefs . . . but back to the shooting contest at the Grand. The bagman paid up and no one complained.

In the wee small hours of the morning as our choppers took off and some of our drivers went to collect our vehicles parked in the hotel grounds, an MP approached Newman and excitedly informed him that the roads between Saigon and Bien Hoa had been cut and that there were VC all over the place. He wanted to know whether the Task Force still intended to drive on to Long Hai. 'Hell yes,' someone answered. 'At least we won't have to go looking for the bastards.'

Along with other Vietnamese elite, Madame Ngo Dinh Diem

had a villa off the beach in the mountains of Long Hai which was an uncontested area firmly in control of the VC. Months earlier, when Gritz had approached the province chief to acquire some land for a fortified camp, the chief had readily accepted, fully believing that these crazy people in tiger suits would not be able to secure any part of Long Hai.

Under a full moon, Gritz had swum ashore one night off a borrowed CIA landing craft and reconnoitred the deserted buildings and grounds. He confirmed that while the VC passed through the area, the site was not occupied. Colonel Hayes provided a battalion of Chinese Nung mercenaries who became the garrison troops and within a week the Task Force had established a base camp. The VC never contested our presence. I suspect that each of us used Long Hai as a recreational area and left the other alone, although the 1st Australian Task Force at Nui Dat had some monumental battles within spitting distance of our camp.

24 A DIFFERENT ARMY IN A DIFFERENT WORLD

Marauder had found a bonanza in enemy documents. The patrol had managed to pull out 80 pounds of paperwork that Newman had stuffed into four haversacks: signals operating instructions, codebooks, one-time message pads, base camp locations and orders of battle. I later found out that the crypto information was so valuable that it was flown to the National Security Agency in Washington. The orders of battle showed that we had broken into the Doan 80C dispensary, which had over 300 patients in it, as well as the Regimental headquarters of the 80th NVA Training Regiment and the 82nd Rear Services Group. The regimental headquarters had apparently shared the facility with an arm of the Central Office for South Vietnam— COSVN. The information was deemed so important that it was sent to the National Security Council. Now this alone would have made the intelligence fraternity sit up and take notice. Between 22 February and 14 May 1967, 22 US and four ARVN battalions had searched War Zone C for COSVN. While most of COSVN was located in the general area of the Mimot rubber plantation in the Fish Hook, Picnic II had uncovered a vital element on the Vam Co Dong in an area to the south, known as the Elephant's Ear. It's therefore within the realms of possibility that Bernie Newman may have spent quality time in General Thanh's personal crapper! I always thought Bernie was a celebrity. The documents also showed that the 141st VC Regiment was in close proximity. The fact that Sunday 7 January was a training holiday and the majority of the battalions were in Cambodia on stand-down was a stroke of luck for which I'm eternally grateful. Unbeknown to us the documents also showed that there was a major push planned against Bien Hoa and Saigon in the period 30–31 January to coincide with the Vietnamese Lunar New Year festivities of Tet.

Based on these revelations, a US division was immediately dispatched to the Vam Co Dong as a pre-emptive strike force. Just kidding. In fact absolutely nothing was done about the regiments massing on the Cambodian border. The divisions around Saigon and Bien Hoa were as thick as blowflies on road-kill, but none were made available to do any real down-and-dirty soldiering.

On 29 January the Task Force moved its FOB to Hao Nghia province for operations on the Kim Bobo and Kim Ghai canals that led into Saigon. I was on leave and was in the capital on the eve of Tet in the company of Harry Lovelock and a few other Australian members of the Team. We were seated in the roof-garden lounge of the Embassy Hotel, drinking Australian beer—nectar of the gods—when the conversation was interrupted by the sound of fireworks. I had winced reflexively. The distant sound was for all the world like small-arms fire. Lovelock had smiled at me. 'You've been in the bush too long,' he said, and sheepishly I returned to the business at hand, which was the demolition of a carton of Fourex. An hour or so later there were more fireworks, only this time in addition to the rattle and pop there were distinct explosions. 'Those are B-40 rockets,' I said and made my way to the balcony. While my drinking companions continued to appear sceptical, their smiles at my discomfiture had grown a little wooden.

From the balcony there's an uninterrupted vista of downtown Saigon, including the US Embassy and the Palace. Uneasy and apprehensive, it dawned on me that what I was seeing were fans of green tracer ricocheting off the streets below, and the star flash of exploding rockets. There were numerous fires in the Cholon district. Within half an hour we were besieged in the hotel, unable to move beyond the mezzanine level while a battle raged on our doorstep.

Years later, Gritz filled me in on what I had missed while I was languishing on the rooftop of the Embassy Hotel:

> We were pinned in a portion of downtown Saigon by an NVA machine-gun team firing from a doorway. Kim Jane was with me. She came up with an idea which blew me away. Trading her tiger suit for a traditional Vietnamese ao dai at the nearest house from which we were taking cover, she tucked her .45 automatic into the band of her silk trousers and headed down the street. Despite my warnings, she ran around the block coming on the machine-gun post from the opposite direction. The surprised NVA soldiers lived long enough to feast their eyes on what they thought was just another beautiful Saigon prostitute. That day Kim earned the respect of every member of the Task Force.

Over the years I've tried to reconcile the events of the Tet Offensive. Given that Rapid Fire had provided Top Secret and accurate intelligence regarding the enemy offensive planned to commence three weeks later, how come we were all so surprised when it happened? Or *was* it a surprise to everyone? What the hell was the National Security Council going to do with the information? Mount a parachute reaction force on the Vam Co Dong from Washington? Of course I'm just being facetious, but seriously, beyond providing an opportunity for a bunch of three-piece suits to point-score in Washington, what the hell *were* they going to do?

And what about the power struggle in Saigon? Westmoreland was the four-star general commanding Macvee. Abrams was his deputy but he was really the king-in-waiting, about to take over, and he had his own staff who jealously guarded what intelligence they could glean, awaiting the moment when Westmoreland stepped down.

In Stanley Karnow's book *Vietnam: A History*, Karnow writes:

> Sam Adams, then a young CIA analyst, later accused Westmoreland and his staff of scaling down estimates of Communist strength (prior to the Tet outbreaks) in an attempt to justify their contention that they were making progress in the war.

Next came Weyand, commander of all the legions of Two Field Force Victor, with his own staff. The four haversacks full of documents would no doubt have gone to the Combined Documentation Exploitation Center under Weyand's jurisdiction, so his senior staff must have known what was going on. So, why, in the small hours of that morning, a full three weeks after the documents' arrival, were the legions of the Free World in cluster-fuck around their bases while the Embassy and the Palace were being besieged? Why were the enemy regiments on the Vam Co Dong left to their own devices to pursue their plans? Those thoughts reminded me of the conversation between Gritz and Colonel Hayes at the time the Task Force had demolished the Cao Lac Bo at Bien Hoa. Bo Gritz had said that he was in a different army, fighting a war in a different world. I hark back to Hayes' comment about being in the unreal world and his admonishment to Gritz to get back to the jungle, the real world.

So, what have we got? Three-piece-suited parachutists from

Washington, two suspicious warlords in Saigon and the mighty cluster-fucking legions—a different army fighting a war in a different world? Years later I was confronted by a career crisis, and while the circumstances were dissimilar the notion of a different army prevailed. I hadn't seen Ron Grey since Rapid Fire days. He had been promoted to major general and was in the process of taking up an appointment as the Chief of Operations in Canberra. I was a major in Personnel Branch, shuffling paper.

So onerous were my duties that to relieve the pent-up tension I co-authored a paper which I called 'A Force Structure: The Bi-Mobile Force Concept for the Army'. Bill Houston, my fellow author, also languishing in Personnel, was an expert in weapon systems and together we hit on a concept that was eminently workable. The thrust of the paper was simply this: because the Australian Army would always have a manpower shortage in any conflict, it must adopt a 'force multiplier' approach. Houston and I researched the latest technologies in infrared heat-seeking, laser-beam riders and TV guidance systems. And this was in 1977, thirteen years before Desert Storm!

I had bumped into General Grey quite by accident one day in the damp corridors of Army Office at Russell. He wanted to know what I was doing and I told him about the paper. He was enthusiastic and wanted to see it. Having read it, he asked me to delay the paper's publication in the *Army Journal* as he had other plans for it. Two weeks later my phone rang and it was Grey. The somewhat one-sided conversation went something like this: 'Do you realise you're regimentally undressed?' I was totally flummoxed. 'Sir . . . ?' I managed to spit out. I darted a glance at the half-length mirror conveniently fixed in the corridor just in front of my office. My polyester uniform looked okay . . . fly done up . . . 'Since when does a lieutenant colonel get away with wearing a major's crowns?'

My mind was reeling but Grey didn't give me a chance to gather my thoughts. 'I want you up here in Operations Branch,' he growled. 'When?' I responded woodenly. 'Yesterday. Get out of that shit-box you're in and up to Ops branch right now. You know where it is? You need a compass?' There was a pause and I detected a chuckle. 'You better go via the Quartermaster's store and fix up your rank. Congratulations.'

The plan Grey had for the paper was to use it as a basis for discussion at the coming Chiefs of the General Staff exercise to be held at Canungra. I was over the moon. Here was an opportunity for Houston's and my theories to be road-tested by the most senior professionals of the Australian Army, not to mention my own heady entry into the fast lane. I couldn't sleep at night, mentally reworking the scenarios I had plotted for the foundation of our force structure. 'You're too junior to be a member of the directing staff at the exercise,' Grey told me with an undertone of excitement in his voice, 'but I want you to go to Canungra and do some "pencilling" for some of the syndicates. It'll give you some idea of what the generals are thinking.' This was even better! I was being given an opportunity to gain first-hand experience of the thought processes of the army's privileged few. At the same time I was apprehensive of the scrutiny that my concept was about to come under.

The key force structure question revolved around the deployment of fire support systems against a background of an enemy invading northern Australia. It was set in a medium intensity war setting. To prompt discussion at grass-roots level the scenario was pitched where a Lance missile was launched way behind the combat zone carrying TGSMs—tactically guided sub-missiles—to be released over the battlefield. The TGSMs would then be guided by front line troops carrying lasers. It was a challenging artillery question, breathtaking in its scope. What would be the command and control breakdown? How would you structure the forces on the ground?

The syndicate I was to 'pencil' for was led by an Australian major general and there were two brigadier generals—one Pommie, the other from the US; both having served with NATO—included in the group of six. The Australian syndicate leader had an artillery background and I was confident that pearls of wisdom would pour forth. The syndicate had been given a day to prepare with all the relevant details on latest missile technology available.

The night before had been a dining-in night and the old boys had played up into the small hours of the morning. The road maps in the eyes of the syndicate leader told the story. However the morning was crystal clear, a typical Canungra morning once the mist had burnt off, conducive to clear thinking. I listened with bated breath as the syndicate leader cleared his throat and blearily addressed the problem. 'I don't know much about any of this,' the general grumbled, casting aside the paper with the question on it. 'I tell you what. It was a good night though, wasn't it? Last night?' The general's sickly smile brought a chuckle of agreement from the rest of the group. The general beetled his brow, obviously trying hard to concentrate through the fog that his wine-soused brain was floating in. 'Anyhow . . . all this missile stuff leaves me cold. But I tell you what I can do . . .' He brightened up at the prospect of dealing with something that was at least remotely relevant. 'I can tell you a story. When I was in Malaya during the emergency, oh back in . . . '59 I guess? We fired that 105 mm pack howitzer over some of the steepest ridgelines you can ever imagine . . .'

I was gobsmacked. I couldn't believe what I was hearing. The old boys were now deep into comparisons—Korea versus Malaya versus Sukarno's Confrontasi. The two one-star generals from NATO who had hitherto shown real interest in the question were now actively participating in the bullshit session and the directing staff smiled along benevolently. But that wasn't the worst of it. The death knell was sounded five days later, during the wind-up. It came in the form of a presentation with bells and whistles attached. It was aptly called 'Man, the Measure of All Things'. I was struck by the slick production. There were film clips from the battle of the Somme, shots of the Fuzzy-Wuzzy Angels on the Kokoda Trail, etc., all of it designed to indicate that in the final analysis it's man's courage and fortitude that carries the day. Suitable music . . . much applause . . . the old boys uplifted, happy once again to be on familiar ground. I ground my teeth, wondering whether I had the courage to speak up. To mention the fact that Gallipoli was a major fuck-up on the part of the British Navy, that the killing grounds of the Somme and Fromelles of Flanders Field would never had occurred had competent generals *not* deployed Allied troops into the face of German machine-guns that mowed them down in their thousands, and that this was the whole point of a new force structure to facilitate new weapons technology. To save lives! But my courage failed me. I sat despondently amidst the audience which clapped enthusiastically. They'd won the day, these poor sad ultra-conservative 'old boys' who would now return to their various commands to reinvent the wheel and prepare to fight the next war using the strategies of the last one. The unspoken conclusion to the exercise was that the concept was grandiose—in the realms of 'Star Wars'. With that, Grey's own star waned. He was never given the appointment of army chief. Indeed he spent his last active years as the Commissioner of Federal Police.

It saddens me to think that this man of courage, intellect and capacity was sent to contemplate his navel or whatever it is that being 'sent out to pasture' means. Yes indeed, I was in a different army, and the army that surrounded me was in a different world.

25 THE SPARK OF ZEUS

And Bo Gritz fared no better. In mid-1979 my battalion officers' mess was scheduled to have a dining-in night and the adjutant had approached me late one afternoon when we were about to shut up shop for the day. 'Who do you want to invite as the guest of honour, Sir?' he'd asked. I hadn't thought about it much, and on impulse I said, 'Invite Bo Gritz.' Well now, my every word was law and this was immediately translated as a staff directive. The battalion intelligence officer was given the task of tracing Gritz's whereabouts. A week later the IO appears before my desk, salutes smartly and says: 'Sir, as you know I've been trying to trace Bo Gritz. Well, I've got these people in my office, they say they're from some aircraft company in the States . . . they're giving me a hard time wanting to know why I'm looking for him. They don't seem to believe me when I tell them I want to invite him to a dining-in night!' I maintain a stern face, but a chuckle bubbles just below the surface. Bo is a free spirit and would think nothing of coming to Australia to meet up with an old comrade, but to these CIA spooks— and I assume that's who the 'aircraft company' people are—the invitation would appear highly suspicious.

In fact I later found out that Gritz, while serving within the Office of the Secretary of Defense in Washington, had been given immediate retirement so that he could search for American POWs in Southeast Asia. His cover was the Hughes Aircraft Company in El Segundo, California. For the next few years he conducted covert operations throughout Thailand, Laos and Cambodia, culminating in a highly secret meeting with Khun Sa, the drug warlord of Burma, in 1986. Khun Sa's Nationalist Chinese Army soldiers had escaped Chairman Mao's takeover of China in '49 and established themselves in the depths of the Burmese jungle, proclaiming their territory as the Shan State. Khun Sa's Shan State was the chief heroin producer in the Golden Triangle. The US government had a report that Khun Sa had information on POWs which he was prepared to divulge on the proviso that the United States recognised the Shan State as a separate nation.

Apparently when Gritz finally located Khun Sa he quickly realised that there was no basis to the report about US POWs, but with great aplomb Khun Sa played an ace which left Gritz dumbstruck. The drug warlord had proposed that, in return for recognition of the Shan State, he would stop the sale of 900 tons of heroin scheduled to flow to the free world, as well as supply the names of every US government official he had dealt with—officials, he claimed, who had been his best customers—for the past twenty years! Reeling from the revelations, Gritz passed this information on to his superiors expecting a positive response, but instead he was told to forget everything he'd heard and erase all the information he had videoed and taped. He was threatened that if he failed to do so he would get 'fifteen years as a felon': five years on a passport charge; five years for transporting explosives; and five years for violating the *Neutrality Act–USA*. In his book he has this to say about the charges: 'I was guilty of all counts. I had been ten times behind Communist lines since 1982, and I never once asked permission of the enemy. I had trained the Afghans and was glad of it. I had used a false passport during the 1986 and 1987 trips into Burma. There was not a single act for which I was afraid to face a jury of my peers.'

Gritz was indicted. His defence was that he had specifically been sent by the White House to Burma and had used a false passport during the mission as part of the covert operation. And that the only reason he was in this pickle was because he had uncovered drug trafficking by certain senior bureaucrats responsible for bringing US POWs home. Gritz alleged that these bureaucrats had misused their offices of POW recovery to traffic in illegal drugs to fund covert operations that Congress didn't want to know about, or wouldn't appropriate money for.

The main charge, *misuse* of a passport, was thrown out on a technicality based on the fact that he had used a false passport, *not* a passport of another person. He was eventually acquitted of all charges with the presiding judge stating that, 'While you are acquitted you are not exonerated.' With that Gritz had leapt up proclaiming that he had not yet had an opportunity of stating his case. He was ordered to silence. So much for putting the government on trial.

On the courtroom steps reporters asked the US Attorney William Maddox why the government had spent two years' worth of taxpayers dollars in pursuit of a case they knew they couldn't win. In response Maddox had answered, 'George Bush called me up and told me to get Bo Gritz.'

I remember at the time I was struggling to rationalise my life, mindful of the things we had done during Rapid Fire. The material about Khun Sa and Gritz's recent misadventures only served to exacerbate my problems.

My thoughts turned to the Bodes, the Free Khmer soldiers who stood shoulder to shoulder with us throughout the Rapid Fire missions. In July 1969 Tan Dara Thach, the senior Khmer Serei representative, met secretly with General Lon Nol who was commander of Cambodia's military forces in Phnom Penh. Lon Nol feared the presence of nearly 50 000 North Vietnamese and Viet Cong troops in eastern and north-eastern Cambodia and had been keen to garner the support of the Khmer Serei. Lon Nol was opposed to Prince Norodom Sihanouk's policies towards the communists and thus an ideal partner for the strongly anti-communist Khmer Serei. At that meeting it was decided that the Special Forces-trained Khmer Serei would bolster the poorly trained 32 000 troops under Lon Nol in the overthrow of Sihanouk.

In January 1970 Task Force members were informed of their role in the pending *coup d'état*. In May 1970 the Cambodians of the Task Force were flown out of Long Hai aboard US Air Force C-130 aircraft, their destination Phnom Penh's Pochentong Airport. Shortly after arriving, they were heavily engaged in battles with the North Vietnamese troops. Over the next few months, the Task Force Khmer Serei troops were integrated into the Cambodian Army.

By 1975 the Khmer Rouge had taken over in Cambodia and were systematically tracking down and murdering all supporters of Lon Nol, and that included the Khmer Serei. Most of the Task Force Cambodians either perished in the battles against the North Vietnamese or were subsequently culled in the Khmer Rouge killing fields. So, what were the ethics of all this?

I went in search of answers within the Christian faith.

Most people speak of Christianity as if it were a unified entity, which of course it isn't. Christianity covers a broad spectrum from fringe congregations and contemporary sects like the Unification Church of the Reverend Moon through various denominations of Protestantism to the 'orthodoxies' of Henry VIII's Church of England and finally Roman Catholicism. The single factor linking these divergent creeds is the New Testament, which purports to be the literal word of God but in fact is a series of revised writings by four men over a period up to 100 years after the death of Christ. One of these men was a Greek doctor who composed his work for a highly ranked Roman official in Caesarea, the Roman capital of Palestine. The Roman regime was brutal and autocratic, so I was not surprised to find no criticism of Rome in these writings, which portrayed the inhabitants of Judaea as placid and contented. Yet when Mark's Gospel was composed, Judaea was in open revolt and thousands of Jews were being crucified, pointing to the fact that the Gospels were obviously written to impress a Roman readership.

In theory, Christianity values highly the sanctity of life, but what about in the ancient past? Now I'm no theologian, but it seems to me that the Spanish Inquisition and the various crusades against the Arab 'infidels', all in the name of the Holy Church, serve to substantiate my doubts. In more recent times religious persecution at an unprecedented level occurred in Bosnia in World War II where the Ustase, fervent Roman Catholics, set about liquidating the Greek Orthodox Church. Orthodox villages were sacked and their inhabitants massacred. Orthodox churches were burnt down, often with the screaming congregations inside them. So, in general, wars are tolerated as long as they are 'good': that is, sanctioned by the church and the state. Given that both of these entities appear to be flawed, I went in search of a different viewpoint, but was at a loss as to which direction I should travel.

The boardwalk at Laguna Bay has wooden seats, spaced every twenty yards or so, built into the bank and in the early winter mornings the easterly sun beats pleasantly on them. One morning I met Peter on one of his favourite seats, basking in the sun. He's in his seventies and has led an interesting life, having studied for the priesthood when he was young, and then much later becoming a journalist. I enjoy my conversations with him. He has no preconceptions and we have a mutual interest in writing. I mentioned the fact that I had become disillusioned with Christianity and was searching for . . . I guess wisdom. 'We must die, but must we die moaning?' Peter said, and I cut a glance at him to confirm that he hadn't taken leave of his senses. 'Have you heard of the Stoics?' I said that I hadn't. 'It might be worth your while to read Epictetus,' Peter added.

Fired by curiosity, I spent hours trying to trace this Roman philosopher until I finally found what I was after in Abbey's Bookshop in Sydney. I obtained a copy of *The Discourses of Epictetus*, published by Everyman. The book was interesting. The hands-on approach was refreshing and the sheer honesty in the writing was surprising, considering that Epictetus was born a slave in Hieropolis in Turkey, a Greek-speaking province of the Roman Empire. Having been a slave to Epaphroditus, an immensely powerful freedman of Nero, would have placed enormous constraints on what Epictetus could say, but through strength of character he prevailed and his words ring unfettered. Nevertheless he was exiled at the age of 34. His philosophy, it seems, is based on the notion that Zeus has given human beings the power to examine and make correct use of their impressions, but this must be in the context that they recognise that everything which happens and which is not 'up to us' is subject to the planning of Zeus. He defines it this way: 'Some things are up to us and others are not. Up to us are opinion, impulse, desire, aversion, whatever is our own action. Not up to us are body, property, reputation, office, whatever are not our own actions.'

This gives us a clue as to what value Epictetus places on life. In his discourse on what is in our power, and what is not, Epictetus says: 'But what says Zeus? "Oh Epictetus, if it were possible, I would have made this poor body and property of yours free and not liable to hindrance. But as things are, you must not forget that this body is not your own, but only cleverly moulded clay. Since, then, I could not give you this, I have given you a certain portion of myself, this faculty . . . to act and not to act, and desire and aversion . . . If you attend to this you will never be restrained, never be hindered. You will not moan . . ."'

And then I read the segment where Epictetus tells the story of how Florus, a Roman historian, was summoned by Emperor Nero to perform in one of his so-called tragedies. Nero delighted in forcing, at pain of death, famous Romans to dress up and act out degrading roles on stage.

'Hence Agrippinus, when Florus was considering whether he should go to Nero's shows so as to perform, said to him: "Go." . . . "So why did you not go yourself?" said Florus. "Because," replied Agrippinus, "I do not even consider doing so." For as soon as a person even considers such questions . . . he draws close to those who have lost all sense of their proper character . . . "But if I do not, I shall lose my head." "Go and act it then, but I for my part will not."'

And like Agrippinus, Bo Gritz, on that fateful day when he was issued his warning at pain of fifteen years' penal servitude did not hesitate. There was nothing to consider; he would proceed. The spark of Zeus was truly with the warrior and all I can say is that once upon a time I had the privilege to stand beside such a man. Instead of venerating a highly decorated patriot of impeccable character, his government has vilified him by branding him a charlatan and has left him beleaguered in his own country.

26

REFLECTIONS IN PARADISE

I'm brought back from my reverie to the leafy surrounds of Sandy's Delicatessen. Nature calls and at my age I'm disinclined to ignore it. As I stand there with my pecker performing in fits and starts, I can smell cigarette smoke and cast a glance at the cubicle to my right. The door is slightly ajar and as I finish my business I move over to it and push it open. Here's young Ashley sitting on the throne, fully clothed, puffing on a fag. I lean forward and snatch the cigarette out of his mouth. 'Give me that,' I say as I snuff the burning tip between my thumb and forefinger and flick the fag into a wastebasket. Ashley jumps back as if bitten by a snake. 'Go join your mother,' I say as he pushes past me, a look of uncertainty on his face. He moves back hesitantly in the general direction of his mother still seated at her table, his eyes never leaving me. The look he gives me makes me think I must have stepped on a turd or something. I chuckle. It's been a long while since I'd seen anybody look like that at me.

So what's changed? I wondered as I cast a glance in the direction of Ashley and his mother. Simon, the boyfriend, looked as if he wished the kid would disappear so he could climb into the mother's pants. Despite all the complexities of life, it all still boils down to sex and money—getting enough of both, unless of course you're an old man and then you dream about . . . having an uninterrupted stream. I turned the pages of the newspaper spread on the table before me and thought about the one thing that brings tranquillity to my existence.

I love the beach. It has been my salvation. It is like a capricious woman whose whims are as complex as the ocean that breaks upon it is deep. I love its contented nature when fluffy white clouds dance across a bright blue sky and little waves frolic. My love is no less potent when its mood changes from contentment to dark-eyed treachery and a shore dump crashes, sending spray like soapsuds in the air; or in the early morning when the weather moves in from the south-east and the cloudbank is the colour of old bruises and the sea looks like pewter in the struggling sunlight.

One March day in 1969 Pop died. Mister George was apparently about to telephone me at Scheyville when he saw me walking into the garage. On that morning the sky was leaden. It was as if nature itself was mourning Pop's passing. There was a terrible ache inside of me. I mourned Pop's death, but there was more to my feelings than just that. I felt that I had let him down. Shirley and I were already in Brisbane under somewhat irregular circumstances. Indeed I was half expecting a visit from the military police and was even entertaining the possibility of being the star performer at a court martial.

'You know, he was a soldier to the end,' Mister George said after he'd told me of Pop's death. 'Died to attention,' he added, his eyes brimming over. Apparently Pop had climbed onto a chair to get at some blankets from the top of a wardrobe when a heart attack took him. He fell backwards and landed stiffly to attention, where he was found a few hours later. Pop had no money. His legacies were the fond memories he left behind. He was a kind and good man uprooted by a revolution that had turned family and friends against each other. Pop had just retired from his job at the furniture factory and had suddenly found himself alone and vulnerable.

A few months earlier I had returned from Vietnam and had been given a posting to the Officer Training Unit at Scheyville, a long way from Camp Hill. As well as the army camp near a small town called Windsor, there was an RAAF base at Richmond nearby—another small town with limited resources. Accommodation was scarce. Shirley and I had no children at the time and therefore had very few points towards a local married quarter. I had managed to find a pokey upstairs flat in Windsor. We didn't like it, but there was nothing we could do about it. The flat was in the main street and at night a fluorescent billboard reflected flickering lights on the bedroom wall, disturbing our sleep. It was a real letdown for us, and nothing like what I expected. I had counted the days to my return from active service when I could be with my wife again, and living in a doss-house with rooms the size of a shoebox did nothing for my morale. That fact and the depressing psychedelic night-show made the task of re-establishing marital relationships all that much harder. I was angry, disoriented and jaded. So at the time when Pop needed assistance to readjust to a life in retirement, his only son was found wanting.

I can only surmise how Pop felt. The elderly in Russia had never wanted for succour. The young in the community respected the elderly; families cared for their old folk. There was always a warm place for dedushka or babushka at the fireplace of the yurt. I'm sure Pop had put little thought into what he was going to do when his wages stopped coming. I guess he assumed that I would look after him, and he would have been right in that assumption except that we had had no room for him in our shoebox at Windsor. He was a proud man who would never ask for help and it was up to me to see the problems and make arrangements.

My first week in my new posting had been less than auspicious. I was appointed an instructor on Battle Wing and my first job was to supervise an ambush demonstration for a class of officer trainees. While studying the lesson plan, I was dismayed to find that the demonstration was of an area-type ambush favoured during the Malay emergency where penny-packets of soldiers, grouped into pairs, were scattered within a 100-yard radius in the jungle. It was a concept perhaps workable in circumstances where the enemy groups were small and poorly armed. We were training future platoon commanders to go to Vietnam at the height of the conflict, where the enemy was numerous and very well armed. Patently, the planned ambush demonstration was not only outdated but also dangerous. I made an instant decision, scrapped the lesson plan, rewrote it to follow the technique we used in Rapid Fire operations with left, right and rear security groups set up in a U-shaped pattern. I also introduced the use of claymores to initiate the ambush and break contact. Having done all this, I called a meeting after hours of the sergeant instructors who would be demonstrating the technique, and ran the drills a few times until they were all confident with them. Their enthusiasm was unbounded. Some of the sergeants had been to Vietnam and appreciated the technique.

On the day, I was pleased with the demonstration, but apparently the Chief Instructor was not. He hauled me into his office and proceeded to tear strips off me. I had not discussed the change with my immediate superior, nor had I cleared this 'controversial' technique with the Chief Instructor, and this so pissed him off that he was hoarse by the time he had finished with me. I waited till he ran out of steam and then told him what he could do with his job and stormed out. On my way home to our garret I made a telephone call to the office of the Directorate of Infantry and informed them that I was leaving, and that if anyone wanted to talk to me I would be in Brisbane.

And that of course brings me to Camp Hill and Pop's untimely death.

Anyhow, I met the Director of Infantry the following day at the airport. I am forever indebted to my wife who managed to keep me in check during that meeting, pouring oil on troubled waters and certainly saving my career. Needless to say I was ropeable. The anger I felt over the stupidity of what happened at Scheyville was only made worse by the tragedy of Pop's death. I was numb and in shock and gave the director short shrift. It was a measure of his patience that we concluded our discussion amicably. I was re-posted to the Officer Training Group at Kelvin Grove in Brisbane under the experienced and mature eye of Gil Lucas, who helped me in my process of rehabilitation. Little did I know that while the immediate readjustment to a stable peacetime environment took little time, the deep-seated horrors of the night would remain. I had thought that three decades later I had finally rid myself of them, but apparently not.

But I have my tranquillity, my beach—through all seasons.

On a wintry dawn the beach can be especially magical as dewdrops sparkle in the needles of the she-oaks that line the dunes. In the hush of early morning the surf has that delicious slurpy sound about it, reinforcing the notion that something magical is happening. And there are a number of us, devotees of the beach who brave the early morning chill, kindred spirits in search of that magic. There's Wes and Errol, Lucy and Desley, and Al and Margi, Peter of course, and a dozen more whose names I don't recall but who greet me as a friend. Most of us exercise a little—some more than others—while we imbibe what nature has to offer—simple things that refresh the spirit and cost nothing.

My pleasant thoughts are interrupted as I glance at young Ashley who, I notice, is still scowling at me. I think he's keeping me in mind for future revenge. The mother bird hasn't drawn breath, her useless chatter filling the space. On second thoughts, I think Ashley looks like he's just about reached the right age to start his apprenticeship in 'old people hunting'. Seems to be the trend these days for young blokes to take to old people. You know, rape the odd granny, break into a few flats where old people live, maybe steal some money for dope, that sort of thing. Still, I guess things could be worse. We could be living in the days of ancient Rome. I let my mind wander in that direction, conjuring up pictures of teenagers in Roman togas accosting elderly ladies on their way to the Colosseum. That scene just didn't seem to work. In Agrippinus' day, such an act would have been considered a gross violation of the spirit, the culprits being instantly put to the sword by some member of the elderly person's family. Actually not such a bad idea! Now that I'm on this track, I wonder how the Romans would have handled the 'big finger' salute commonly used today, especially by motorists. You know, the sport of road raging where strangers pump the big finger in a frustrated attempt to make their point regarding some real or perceived wrong done to them by the other party. I think in Agrippinus' day big-finger pumping would have been considered a slight on the other person's spirit that would have led to a duel. A constraining factor, I would think, leading to a much more polite society, and probably a fitter one, given that the men would have to keep up their sword skills. But apparently the Romans, too, had their share of criminally inclined jackasses. Epictetus had this to say about them: 'Some of us become like wolves, faithless and treacherous and noxious; others, like lions, wild and savage and untamed; but most become like foxes, the most roguish of living creatures . . . Take care that you do not become one of those roguish creatures.'

The mother bird gathers up her wallet and sunshades and all three prepare to go, I guess back to the tribal pad. In a way I'm sorry to see young Ashley go. I would have liked some quality time with him; he's not beyond redemption. The strip is getting busy now, all sorts of people walking by—mostly moneyed. Idly I glance at the passing parade—cargo shorts and deck shoes prevail. There are Tommy Hilfigger caps and Calvin Klein sunshades and the birds are into mules and boot-leg hipsters in dark denim or black. Armani sunshades amble past me like a procession of stealth bomber pilots. A chick struts by heading in the direction of Cato's Bar. She looks as though she's just stepped out of the pages of *Fashion Forever*—Italian leather boots, a black Dolce & Gabbana skivvy, bleached blonde hair loosely pulled up with a butterfly clip and a gold Belcher link bracelet that would weigh down an ocean liner. There's a whiff of perfume that follows her like a trailing shadow. The smell is vaguely familiar—Shirley loves her perfumes and often samples the great variety on offer at the chemist shop near Sandy's—I think it's called Hypnotic Poison.

So how has the Vietnam War impacted on these beautiful people? What, for instance, did the slick chick from *Fashion Forever* think about Vietnam? Did she wonder, for instance, whether we as a nation had been involved in the 'good' fight? Why would she? And how could she, when the educational system would not have taught her, and community preferences avoided discussion of the 'ugly' subject of Vietnam?

And in fact, *had* we been involved in the 'good' fight? Of course we had; after all, we fought to preserve a democratically elected and stable South Vietnamese government. I'm joking, of course. But that's the myth the nation was fed. In fact the regime run by Bao Dai, an inveterate gambler and womaniser in cahoots with Diem, a repressive dictator, had not been popularly elected but was hastily cobbled together by the CIA. Various other administrations followed each other into the meat grinder of military coups and shady deals, through which the underlying stench of corruption was always strong. Despite the political rhetoric that elucidated lofty principles of preserving freedom and fair play, the truth is that Australia committed itself to a war in Vietnam simply to cadge favours from the United States. There was the memorable blank-cheque statement made by the then Prime Minister: 'All the way with LBJ.' *That* kneejerker won us the 'brown nose' award among thinking Western nations and the sobriquet of 'lackey' from communist North Vietnam.

Would this spiffy lady from *Fashion Forever* care? Would she care if she knew that the CIA tried a similar thing later on in Panama with the closet communist Noriega? Would she waste a moment of her time thinking about these things? I mean, what the hell has this got to do with her beautiful life? Do perfidy and stupidity on the part of politicians and their minders impact in any way on our slick chick? Should they? This lady gives me the impression of being self-assured and aloof, but in her aloofness does she have any understanding of what's going on around her beyond the facade of her existence? In any event, how *does* humanity handle the madness of war? I conjure up a picture of a child who spots an ant trail in the garden, and out of mischief or whimsy squashes a few hundred of them with her thumb. What are the effects? At first the surviving ants rush about aimlessly, but then they resume their orderly movement carrying crumbs and whatnot along the trail as though nothing has happened.

So, *our* ant trail has re-established itself and we're pressing on with the business of living. Slick chick is about to disappear into Cato's Bar, her hips swinging in that breathtakingly well-oiled motion of youth . . . Anyhow, back to my original train of thought.

What of Vietnam itself? A generation after the Communist tanks had rolled into Saigon, today's post-war Vietnamese baby-boomers, over 50 per cent of the population, also seem to know very little about the war and couldn't care less about it. Those who were old enough to remember have hazy memories of bombs, the stuff of nightmares. The capitalist society that so abhorred North Vietnam's communism now seduces it for its own entrepreneurial ends. South Korea, which had 25 000 troops deployed in Vietnam fighting the communists, now has huge oil and gas interests in that country, a stake amounting to billions of dollars. The United States and Australia, which have long since stopped eating humble pie, are expanding their trading ties while the government of Vietnam is also adjusting, becoming less trenchant in its policies towards the West. The money trough has been re-formed and the pigs, formerly protagonists, are now face to the trough—cheek by jowl.

So how did Project Rapid Fire fare in all of this? At the time it had been inconceivable to think of the Task Force without Gritz, but in March 1968 he was re-posted and it was as if the sky had fallen in on us. We became vulnerable. It was obvious that the guitar players and ballad singers of Bien Hoa had finally gained the ascendancy: we were given a role of reconnaissance in force in Hau Nghia province, an area as bare and flat as a billiard table. Exposed in open country and without heavy weapons, the conduct of such operations would be suicidal for the Task Force. I said so in no uncertain terms and was reassigned to another job for my troubles. It gave me some satisfaction that after a few weeks the Task Force was eventually moved to Song Be, but it never recovered from the loss of its leader. In my eyes, Bo Gritz stands in the company of legends like Stirling of the British SAS and Popski of Popski's Private Army. About this time, Weyand had dubbed B-36 'the last of the bare-knuckle outfits', an apt description not only because of its connotations of courage and toughness, but because it also represented an anachronism. Like the bare-knuckle gladiators of old, B-36 was I suppose no longer palatable to the New Age thinking of the 90s, but what of post-September 11? Has any part of Gritz's legacy survived?

Not so long ago, while researching my material for this story,

I asked Bo Gritz by email what had happened to him when he left B-36. This is what he had to say:

> My final mission was to have involved the capture of an NVA General, the artillery commander of South Vietnam. He moved north after the French Indochina War in 1954, but his traditional family home was in the flat rice basket area in the Plain of Reeds west of Can Tho. CIA signal intercepts indicated the General was visiting his parents. Spy plane photos showed a French-style house surrounded by trees, and what looked like an armed guard of about thirty soldiers. A bomb shelter was located some 150 meters beyond. A stream ran by the property which joined others and flowed into the South China Sea. VC battalions encircling the location provided an outer ring of security against attack.
>
> I was called to II FFV at Long Binh and given the mission to capture the General. My plan was simple. Major Ron 'Smokey' Barnes, our Forward Air Controller, would fly at 12,000 feet to attract no ground attention. An observer using binoculars would guide two slicks flying low to the target. The lead bird would go in with guns blazing and crash through the roof. The second ship would provide cover and land at the shelter—just in case the general had moved. My team would lift off with the prize, or if our Huey was damaged in the initial penetration, the back-up ship would fly the general out. Stand-by troops would provide close support as required. Smokey would have TAC aircraft in orbit for close air support to keep reinforcements from interferring.
>
> General 'Red' Fuller was General Fred Weyand's operations chief. During my brief back he exploded, 'You Special Forces think you can kill anybody! Haven't you ever heard of the MACV Rules of Engagement? You cannot open fire until you are receiving fire!' The following exchange was blunt and brutal. I told Fuller that the only way to gain surprise was with

a small lightning strike force, with a large reserve to exploit if needed. I wouldn't compromise our lives or the mission for anyone's 'rule book'.

Shortly after the altercation with General Fuller, a fatherly Fred Weyand, promoted to four stars, and destined to become COMUSMACV, called me to his office. 'Bo, I'd like to get your comments on a letter I recently received from General Robert York, CG of the Infantry Center at Fort Benning, Georgia,' he said.

General York was offering to provide Weyand with two equipped and trained American Ranger Battalions. I was ecstatic. 'Sir, this is great news. Use them as one-two punches in each of the War Zones. One is preparing while the other is deployed. They will do the close combat work of more than an infantry division.'

'That's what I thought, but my staff tells me we just can't support any more combat troops right now,' Weyand replied.

'My God, Sir, send the Big Red One or Old Reliables (9th Infantry Division) home!'

Weyand pulled a sad face. 'I hear you, but Bo, there's something else I wanted to talk to you about. I want you to come up on my general staff. Use this war to get ahead of your contemporaries. You're just going to get yourself killed trying to win.'

I was shocked. 'Sir, I know I can't win the war by myself, but don't we all have to do our best every day so that some day we can justify all the loss of limbs, liberty, and lives of those who did try?'

Weyand looked kindly at me and said, 'Bo, we aren't going to win this war.'

His words brought the world down around me. I had sacrificed my family, I was prepared to lay down my life! This was my life! The men, our missions, the Task Force was the only existence I cared about. Without them, I was dead. It seemed that everyone in authority had tried to destroy the most perfect body of warriors ever assembled since we were created. Colonel John G. Hayes, CO of III Corps Special Forces, was constantly trying to pull me out of the field for fear I would be killed. Why wouldn't these soldiers let us alone to fulfill our purpose on this earth?

I decided that day that I wouldn't be responsible for another drop of GI blood in Southeast Asia. Like a gambler just trying to get even, I cut my losses and came home—to a strange place where it seemed I no longer belonged.

I glance about me. Some of the magic has faded from the morning. Time to move on, but what about the sacrifices? What do you say to the ghosts? To those who laid down their lives in the killing grounds of War Zone C? Sorry, my friend, but you were duped? You sacrificed your life pointlessly, and no one really cares? But that's not true, they've put up memorials and once a year a whole bunch of old people gather to reminisce. The trouble is, every time I think of that my mind slips to the picture of that re-formed trough and all those pigs slopping it up, cheek by jowl . . .

I fold my paper, climb out of my chair and head down Hastings Street towards the beach. Cirrus clouds have gathered and the sun is a fuzzy glare in the north-east—a mackerel sky. I'm glad of the cool conditions, they keep many of the tourists from the beach. I increase the pace, my bare feet tracking in the wet sand. My thoughts return to my nightmare and an idea pops into my mind: perhaps the face has come back in the night to tell me that I should write this story, to leave an imprint of . . . what? The madness of war? Mendacity? I think the face would want me to simply tell the story, to try and justify the sacrifice. To somehow make amends. I hope I've got it right. I dread the shadows on the wall.

EPILOGUE

EPILOGUE

Beyond the shadows on the wall there are some sights and sounds that sort of live within my mind, unwelcome baggage that shares my space. Sometimes on a dreary winter's day I hear the distant mewling of seagulls. I see them picking over a piece of storm wrack on the beach, but the sound they make reminds me of something else. I don't want to be reminded of that sound, but no one's given me a choice. I know the sound; it comes from beyond my tranquil setting. It comes from the jungle.

There's pandemonium in the jungle. The snarl of automatic weapons fire pierces the stillness and gunsmoke hangs in little pockets at ground level. I see a Bode slumped against the broad base of a tree. He just sits there, mewling. The medic has tended to him and has now crawled away in search of others who urgently need his ministrations. The Bode knows that he is dying. His lifeblood is seeping from him and he can do no more than slump against that tree while madness takes its course around him. There's another Bode, no more than a dozen feet from the first. This one has shucked off his webbing and he's voraciously eating, grimy fingers shovelling a mixture of little sprat-like fish mixed with rice. He's not doing this because he's greedy or insensitive, but because he needs an energy fix. The battle has sapped him and now he has temporarily found a little place of sanity where he can shelter from reality while he restores himself.

There's another sound, a feeble voice that quavers and can only be heard periodically over the rattle and pop of firing. It's a 'round-eye'—we called ourselves that as opposed to 'slope' or 'slope-head'—how's that for political incorrectness! The man is calling for a medic. It's a plaintive call tinged with shock and repugnance. Strange, but I didn't hear it then. Now it goes through me like a dagger.

These are some of my sights and sounds and they would not differ greatly from those of the firefighters and policemen on duty at the World Trade Center on that fateful day of September 11. Sadly too, those sights and sounds will remain with them until the day they die.

So what's happened since the fall of the Taliban regime in Afghanistan? Osama bin Laden has been captured and his key subordinates with him. No. I won't say I told you so; I don't wish to boast. In any event some progress has been made. In the first phase of the war (October–December 2001), improvisation was the rule and the Special Forces teams followed in the footsteps of those who had set the scene in Vietnam. The results were phenomenal. With the insertion of a few teams, the Northern Alliance went from controlling fifteen per cent of the country to 90 per cent in a matter of days. The dawning realisation of success apparently brought the headquarters rushing to the field to bask in victory (my sources on the ground are impeccable), and this led to the friendly-fire accidents. All of this reinforces the notion that more normal men only stand in the way of warriors who, when left to their own devices, will achieve the impossible.

And now to those who chose to raise the sword against

innocent people. One hundred and fifty or more members of the al-Qaeda network are being held as prisoners and are being interrogated at the Guantanamo Bay US naval base in Cuba. Some British politicians are making strong noises about the human rights implications of holding prisoners, hooded and manacled, in outdoor cages open to the weather. Amongst the captured al-Qaeda are members of nationalities other than of a Middle Eastern nature. Some may end up in a military commission, others in the US criminal system, perhaps even in Australia. But already there are people clamouring for leniency, demanding their immediate return home without further interrogation. Forget the abominations . . .

I think of Vietnam, reflecting briefly on those days of stacked magazines and . . . and the tiger's baleful eye. So who's right? Should we perhaps support the accommodating view, preferring to blot out what happened on September 11 and get on with life? My thoughts turn to the spiffy lady strutting into Cato's Bar. Despite the terrible toll, has she learnt from the experience? Has she got a fuller view of life? Has her perspective changed? Does she see the tiger's baleful eye? Perhaps it's worthwhile to take stock, to revisit momentarily the two towers of the World Trade Center, to picture the sights and sounds.

It's 8.45 a.m. and American Airlines Flight 11 slams into the North Tower. Seventeen minutes later United Airlines Flight 175 crashes into the South Tower. Fed by jet fuel from these two trans-continental aircraft used as weapons, smoke fills the Manhattan sky. The South Tower is the first to collapse, at 10.05 a.m., but before it does so observers watch in horror as frantic people leap from the burning building. A woman falls, horror frozen on the rictus of her face. Twenty-three minutes later the North Tower implodes in a storm of dust, smoke, and particles of concrete and steel, taking with it the shredded bodies of those trapped inside.

Surely that is the measure of the tiger against which civilised man must gauge his responses. Or should we close our eyes to the horror of that moment and pray that peace will come with forgiveness, and there will be no more need for Rapid Fire. No more . . .

Noosa, March 2002

BIBLIOGRAPHY

Baigent, Michael, Leigh, Richard & Lincoln, Henry, *Holy Blood, Holy Grail*, Delacarte Press, New York, 1982

Chapman, F. Spencer, *The Jungle is Neutral*, Time Life, Virginia, 1988

Donahue, James C., *Blackjack-33*, Ivy Books, New York, 1999

Duiker, William, *Ho Chi Minh*, Allen & Unwin, Sydney, 2000

Fall, Bernard, *Street Without Joy*, Stackpole Books, London, 1965

Gill, Christopher (ed), *The Discourses of Epictetus*, Everyman, London, 1998

Gritz, Bo, *Called to Serve*, Lazarus Publishing Company, Nevada, 1991

Karnow, Stanley, *Vietnam: A History*, Random House, London, 1994

Long, George, *Enchiridion, Epictetus*, Promentheus Books, New York, 1991

Yedinak, Steven M., *Hard to Forget*, Ivy Books, New York, 1998

1443481R0

Printed in Great Britain by
Amazon.co.uk, Ltd.,
Marston Gate.